Embracing No Other

To John,

Best Wishes

Will

Embracing No Other

awakening through shamanic plant medicines
to non-dual awareness of no-self

by
Will Brennan

Tobar Trua

Copyright © 2013 Will Brennan
www.embracingnoother.com

Published by Tobar Trua, 2013
Dromahair, Leitrim, Ireland
www.tobartrua.ie

All rights reserved. No part of this book may be reproduced or utilized in any form or by any means, electronic or mechanical, including photocopying, recording, or by any information storage and retrieval system, without the prior permission in writing from the publisher.

ISBN: 978-0-9926331-0-3

Front cover photograph by Niamh Dempsey
Cover design by Will Brennan and Niamh Dempsey

I am deeply grateful to Stephen for his editorial suggestions and to all those who had a hand in bringing this book to fruition.

With special thanks to Niamh for the love, grace and strength.

Contents

Introduction 1
Something is not right 7
Turning worm and world as one 21
Plant sentience 35
Singing to the drums 45
Betwixt and between 59
The silent voice of Truth 71
Nothing goes unseen 79
Retiring from imagined control 91
No self, no other 105
Losing identity 117
No guilt without pride 127
The infinite mystery chooses 135
My altar is emptied 141
Un-possessed radiance 151
Flowering home 161
'I am' the love song of divinity 171
Nothing is as it appears 181
Our heart 187

Author's Note 197

Introduction

The beginning can be such an elusive point to pin down, especially when it has been seen that there is no true beginning. So how then does one begin to write about the realisation of the illusory 'me'? Perhaps from this very moment itself, which happens to be the very same moment that you are reading these words.

I find myself in the curious and mysterious position of not being the person I had believed myself to be, indeed, I do not find myself at all. So many years spent to heal myself, to become whole, so to speak, I was a seeker of well-being, happiness and sanity. Alas to no avail, not because there is no true and natural happiness, but simply that the very seeking for it is an actual movement from it; from the inherent beauty that already is, an ever-present truth that is our very being.

In one form or another I had come across spiritual pointers that suggested that we already are what we are looking for. This, however, did not stop me from searching and trying to find happiness. Some sense of wrongness always seemed to propel me towards an imagined state of perfection. Perhaps some movements must run their course until the seed of truth unveils.

What I would like to share with you is the timeless moment when it is seen that there is no seeker—no separate, individual person apart from manifestation—and the subsequent embodiment of this truth wherein there can be a process of harmonisation after an awakening to the reality of our true nature.

Harmonisation sounds like such a wondrous word and can evoke notions of celestial music and butterfly wings, but as beautiful a process as it is, it can also be anywhere from challenging to downright mortifying. It could be likened to a dredging of the depths of one's held beliefs, fears and shadow patterns. Plus, it seems, the more out of tune the refusal to surrender is, the wilder the ride as the resistance of body and mind identification is stripped of its constructed, separate reality.

Here is where much of this book is written from, between the movements of absolute clarity and relative, reactive patterns—the pendulum of non-dual truth blending and encompassing the seeming opposites of absolute and relative together, in an act of unconditional love. Nothing gets left behind, as nothing ever has, or ever will stand apart.

Without giving too much deference to my personal past, I will endeavour to outline the movement through shamanism from the perspective of non-dual awareness. Shamanism was, for several years, my way, a path in which I found great solace and mystery, particularly in the exploration of plant sentience and sacred plant medicines. But for all the beauty of such a path, I was still an individual walking it, a person in a state of division and deep struggle looking for healing. This inner division that I brought to the path was reflected in my understanding of shamanism, in that I felt myself to be an isolated individual seeking wholeness through the help of spirit guides, shamans, power animals and Great Spirit itself. For so long, I had seen myself as separate from these healing forces, but as my understanding deepened I began to tackle directly this very sense of a separate 'I' or 'me' by inquiring into the nature and reality of this assumed separation. I began to find that this 'me' was but a moving pattern of thoughts, memories, beliefs, feelings, emotions and sensations. This very identification with the body-mind pattern was brought into question and the source of 'I' was sought with the questioning,

"Who am I?"

Along the shamanic way one may encounter much fun, drama and pain, not to mention the tests and lures of empowerment. Often with the expansion of consciousness come the reigning subtle guises of ego as it seeks to appropriate 'more for me' and 'more of me.' When I first started shamanic work, a teacher commented on how the pull of money, sex and power waylaid many. I imagine that this is true for many spiritual paths and indeed the path of many is paved with both conscious and unconscious desires which are never truly probed, just acted out in the hope of filling an elusive sense of lacking—a glittering promise of becoming that rarely confronts the sense of lacking, or the one who feels it.

In time, my shamanic worldview deepened as I started to probe the nature of consciousness, which often felt like a dance with a dissolving surrender as I learned to let go of so much of the fearful control that seemed to hold 'me' together. Storming to the surface came a deep questioning of the notion of protection in shamanism and a desire to know,

What in me needs protection?

This orientation to a deeper truth gripped me with a relentless force of integrity that needed to be understood at all costs.

You may find as you read that often, while trying to elucidate the ineffable and indescribable, a flight into the poetic can serve as a more apt pointer than a rigid use of linguistics for, after all, language is but an agreed-upon tool of communication which sways in favour of a dualistic model of subject-object relations.

Yet it may be that the words offered here are scented with the energy and realisation of our natural, open state. When the words are not held too tightly, then the very perfume of truth may orientate you to a remembrance of our home ground, an awareness beyond all description or location.

I would suggest not to take anything here as truth until it has been tasted and found to be true. I am no authority, just a voice in the wind that fades to silence.

Something is not right

Many of us know this feeling, sometimes vague, sometimes screaming out from the very marrow. We can turn from it, numb it, deny it, try to drown it, but still it persists. Resistance to life—what is—was the only way I knew. There are so many ways and means to distract from this gnawing feeling. We can lose ourselves in the outward play of life, in the apparent multitude of forms, pleasures and pains.

For me, there came a time to find what was wrong and, if possible, to fix it. A sensible and pragmatic decision, albeit based on some shaky assumptions. To go into my personal tales of woe would serve no purpose, suffice to say that my history is no better or worse than other tales, but similar in the fact that it engendered feelings of constriction and isolation. I would liken it to an invisible, energetic straight jacket of my own making, padlocked for extra safety.

Ratter than dip my toe into the spiritual world, I dived right in to a ten-day, silent retreat without any prior practice or training. This was not out of pure spiritual courage, it was the fact that it was free of charge and that I would not have to talk to any spiritually-minded people and so avoid having to demonstrate my naivety or fear. It was simply a matter of convenience and protection that was paramount for me. Little did I realise what was to follow—a grappling session with the chaos of my own mind and body patterns.

For the first five days, my body literally shook with the tension while trying to meditate in silence. It became apparent that I had no control over my thoughts and that somehow these thoughts were intimately connected to the body. In one of the meditation sessions, every horror or act of violence I had ever watched on television replayed endlessly in my mind in vivid, graphic detail as I kept bringing my attention back to the breath, time and time again. I could see that just as food provided nutrition to build the body, so too everything I had ever watched and listened to was an ingestion that had informed both mind and body.

Day after day, thoughts and memories were eliciting strong emotions and also manifesting as physical pain in the body. For all the world, the pains felt like knots and the whole body system seemed to be knots within knots held together in a contracting pulse that screamed, 'No.' At times I thought I would implode and as the stereo droned out Sanskrit chants to mark the end of every round, I would be filled with the urge to grab that stereo and smash it to the ground with a resounding, 'No.' A no that was pulled as tight as a hangman's noose. But by some unknown grace something shifted in the very midst of this turmoil.

As I sat in meditation, I heard a bird singing outside of the building. As my attention went to the birdsong, I could no longer tell if the sound of the song was inside me or outside me. There seemed to be no bird singing or person hearing the song, there was just the singing. The boundary of inner and outer gave way, all thoughts gave way as the singing blossomed into a singularity—an awareness that was all and everything at once. The singing was a wave of bliss that was an effortless expression of divinity that knew no boundary. Only the moment before, my body had been wracked with pain, but that pain had simply vanished in this untarnished presence. Somehow it seemed that the bird and I were no other than the awareness of this singing, all seemed to stand naked in this glorious simplicity.

Gradually, a sense of self resumed and the tensions in the body re-initiated. However, the same intensity of discomfort and pain was not there, it was as if they could not be identified with to the same degree. I sat there dumbfounded, not really knowing what had just happened. Yet I could not deny that there had been a cessation of suffering. Of that there was no doubt, as there still pervaded a deep sense of peace with everything feeling deeply okay. I had no real context or understanding in which to frame this experience and the habit of mind is to have everything labelled and framed. The taste of this freedom echoed strongly for days. It reverberated in the silence as a deep peace, especially as I walked in nature. I found that the perception of the surrounding beauty was enlivened as I rested in the present moment.

My mind, however, kept scrambling and scrambling. Something unknown had happened and needed to be dealt with as soon as possible—it was a threat to the mind's supremacy. What had happened I could not say for sure. I wondered was it a foretaste of a fully healed state and something that I could aspire to if I kept meditating. Whatever it was, I wanted to know it and to have it. I can see now how the mind had turned this openness into an event and a desirable event at that.

I approached the meditation teacher in a private session to ask for his advice, thinking that he would confirm the specialness of it all. To my surprise, he told me that it was of no great importance and was simply something that happened as one meditated. He advised me to pay it no heed lest it become a desired goal and to simply keep with the awareness of breath in meditation.

I did not then fully understand the subtlety of his meaning. An identified mind can be such a funny thing; it has the ability to turn most things to its way of thinking. I started to think that if what had just happened was of no importance and just a stage on the path, well then imagine what the end goal must be like! The mind boggled with desire to own, acquire and become. I also felt a little, secret joy that I had been given a special preview of what was to come. At that time I had no clue how the egoic-mind, which could be said to be the identification with the separate sense of self, wove thoughts to create a net of time and space of 'not now,' which could catch ever-subtler prey to strengthen its position of becoming. My ego-mind-self was now donning the mantle of spiritual ego, new and improved with spiritual thoughts that could weave a net as fine as any spider's web.

Yet there remained a lingering aroma of peace for days and weeks after the retreat. I was amazed to see how conditioned and reactive people were and perhaps more amazed at how I had never noticed this before. I noticed that I was not as quick to react unconsciously as I had been before, somehow the silence and awareness had opened up a space to let things be, where the 'me' was not as quick to jump in. It felt as if I was a step back, witnessing events unfold, often with great bemusement that people were so engrossed in dramas that they took to be so real, but which seemed to be but a play. It felt as if there was a bubble of perceptual difference, which removed one from the pull of daily dramas.

Alas, as time passed, I found the bubble burst. Before I knew it, I had resumed my old role and was fully engrossed in honking horns and holding court, the judge was reinstalled in full, reactive patterns. At times I could see my old identity reforming, yet I felt powerless to stop it; it was like a gravitational pull and I was simply too heavy to escape its force. It seemed as if I had lost the peace and calm that was revealed at the retreat. I did not see that it was just covered over by my tightly held beliefs, patterns and ideas that defined me and also defined the world I lived in.

Still though, the taste of freedom lingered and once tasted, the possibility of recapture was there, the spiritual seeker was well and truly established—there was an 'I' looking for a way out and all options were on the table with a peppering of zeal and fervour. I can see now that it was nought but a collection of bound thoughts chasing an idea, all taken to be real in the dream of becoming.

I attended some more silent meditation retreats, each time finding I could sit with greater ease, with less and less inner turmoil and pain. The dissolution that had overtaken me on the first retreat would sometimes begin to unfold again but as soon as I would recognise the forefeeling, my mind would yell, 'This is it,' and try to grasp it. In that very moment I would lose it, it seemed as if any movement to hold it, get it, or own it would result in its loss. I even pretended I did not want it, so as to try entice it, but to no avail. Still the penny did not drop, I simply assumed I was doing it wrong or was not clear enough, or good enough, or ready enough. I could not see that the very trying to own, or hold it was itself the antithesis of dissolution and freedom.

Nevertheless, after each retreat I would feel such a sense of expansion and calmness. This in itself was a blessing, but after each retreat I would watch the same process of re-identification happen. Old habits of anger, jealousy and judging would resurface. To let this expansion take root in daily life seemed like a lifetime's work. I had a daily routine of fixed meditation periods, which were like my 'medicines,' but the practice of fixed time and technique involved such control and discipline that I often felt stifled. I also noticed in some of the long-term meditators a lack of spontaneity and joy—they seemed very under control and restrained. I wondered was there a link between this and the controlled form of meditation they practiced.

I noticed how patterns of behaviour and reaction such as anger, jealousy, pleasure and judging were deeply imbedded in me. Although meditation gave me a degree of calm and well being, these patterns were still at the core and would rise again and again, especially when my meditation practice would slip. It often felt as if I was tied to the practice to keep everything in check. I found that the old, familiar situations from the past tended to resurrect the deepest patterns of identity and reactivity.

Some of the more noticeable patterns, such as drinking alcohol, were deeply woven into the fabric of being Irish, being a young man, being happy and fitting in. These patterns are often culturally conditioned into us, along with family patterns, as learned behaviour. Personal will power alone would not suffice—it could bring about abstinence but the patterns remained as if they were woven into the very fabric of 'me.'

I could see that I could not live permanently in a bubble, cut off from life itself for fear of losing calmness and peace. Social occasions could be most challenging as one was expected to be a certain way. I started to see that people had an image of me and of the way I was, they had me labelled and any deviation from the norm was not always welcomed. In fact, close friends and family had the strongest held image of what I was, they knew 'me.' Often they found it hard to allow me to change, as it threatened their image of me and the relationships we had.

Later, I began to see that people need the security of knowing who you are because, in a way, it tells them who they are; it creates fixed positions of identity and there is a security in that. So any change in you often threatens their sense of self and is frowned upon. I remember returning to my hometown during this period and meeting an old school friend. After two or three minutes talking he simply said,

"What the hell happened to you?"

As if I had been irreversibly transformed into a suspicious, alien stranger that might at any moment try to transform him too. So many friendships and relationships are based on mutual likes or interests but if these fall away for one person, often the friendship fades away too.

I found other people's held images of me suffocating at times, it felt like they were holding 'me' in place. Especially as, at that time, most of the people I knew were not interested in any healing or spirituality.

Any talk of such matters was greeted with a bemused smile of indifference or even condescension.

I started to see that my own sense of personal self was held in place by my beliefs, thoughts and memories; an apparent continuum of conditioning that was constantly reinforced by repetitive attention and identification. All this combined to produce reactions to life that were not spontaneous, but merely a rehashing of the known.

One morning I decided that a holiday from being 'me' was needed. I gave up my job that day and went to live in the countryside, on my own in a tiny caravan with neither electricity nor running water, on the land of a friend who was kind enough to let me be there. It was a time to slow down and pull back. It was a vital breathing space, a time to read, reflect and simply be in nature. I found in the solitude a mirror. When patterns of anger or boredom would surface, I had no one to project them on to, nor did I have any of the normal outlets of distraction. So, in that solitude my attention shifted to looking at the source of these patterns. This was a new step for me, to sit with whatever arose internally, to stay with it rather than lose oneself in a reactive response, which was always an attempt to outrun any true feeling or acceptance.

Nature also proved to be a clear mirror to deeper patterns of my held self and a window into present moment awareness where the first tentative steps into being as I was took place. I could see a flow and rhythm in nature that was never static; it was not locked into the past or desperately trying to be in the future. It unfolded moment by moment with a complexity and harmony that was staggering; animals, plants, sun, rain, wind and earth displaying an act of such creativity and wonder.

As I walked in the forest day by day, I began to appreciate the stillness that seemed to be the canvas for this ever-present beauty, a magical dance of light, colour, smells and sounds that sang of a flow that unfolded in the delight of being. Yet often as I walked, the inner turmoil of mind would punctuate the stillness. Once again I would be back judging a past event or holding a grievance, the mind commentator of 'shoulds' and 'should nots,' regurgitating thoughts of rightness and wrongness. I could see that the more I became identified with such thoughts, the more the stillness and beauty of reflected nature would fade. I would become concretised as a separate, isolated figure moving through my own world of turmoil, divorced from the stillness and beauty that, moments before, was so self evident.

And yet those very moments when the thoughts would subside were priceless, the stillness of the trees seemed to embrace one in the remembrance of some essential nature, as if there was a resonance of commonality in our ground of simply being. I found there was a flow in nature that nurtured expansion more deeply than did my prescribed periods of meditation.

It seemed that there was some key to freedom that was reflected in nature's mystery and I felt an irresistible pull, an affinity of recognition that sang of home. Nature seemed to offer an open secret that was veiled by the blinkered mind, which narrowed the field of consciousness like a trail of breadcrumbs keeps a hungry child's focus lowered from the beauty of the expansive sky.

Towards the end of that summer and my dance with nature, loomed my thirtieth birthday. All of my previous adult birthdays had been alcohol and drug-fuelled blurs of mayhem. This time, one of my friends in Dublin contacted me to say that he had organised a party and night out with other friends to celebrate—invitations were out, all were on board and my attendance was required.

What to do?

Nothing!

I could not go but nearly did. To step back in would be to refuse the inner unfolding at such a delicate time. I sent the response, 'No,' which was an even bigger, 'Yes,' to what was unfolding. On the night of my birthday I sat on my own, looking at the sky and strangely, didn't feel so alone.

I later heard that my birthday party had gone ahead with full debauchery. A photograph of me had been taken from a photo album and brought to the pub. They cheered 'Happy birthday' to it, made jokes to it, took it out dancing and generally showed it a good time. My friends had simply just not wanted to let go of the image they had of me: the show must go on. The sheer lunacy of it makes me smile.

Turning worm and world as one

Through this silent dialogue with nature I began to orient more towards a nature-based spirituality. My night-time dreams turned to what I could only then describe as shamanic, with lucid dreams of animals and beings of a magical nature. I felt I was being called to investigate a new way.

I had no idea what this would entail or how I would go about exploring this magical realm but there was a definite pull towards it. At this time I had returned to college to study Fine Art, for which I had a great love. This, however, necessitated a return to city living and the life situation I was so desperate to change.

Art had been such a find for me. I relished the sense of timelessness that unfolded as I worked on a piece of art. There was a sense of peace and communion as thoughts subsided in the surrender to the flow of work. My mind would be at rest as hours would silently pass by in the blink of an eye. Satisfaction was more in the moment of creativity than in the end result of the finished object of art. I could see that there was a similarity to that timeless flow of creativity, the meditative state and the stillness of nature, but to me at that time it was hit and miss as to whether I could get to that peaceful state. It felt as if I was very much separate from that timeless, aware stillness.

When the flow of creativity would cease, the egoic-mind would step right back in to claim the credit and the doer-ship. It created a sense of ownership—'me' as the artist, basking in praise and fearing criticism—an identity very much rooted in the ideas and beliefs I had of what an artist was. I found that the more serious I became about studying art, the more I became embroiled in the academia of grades, judgments and conditioning—a little game of becoming that squeezed so much of the joy, spontaneity and surrender out of what was natural, silent and present; a game of conditioned becoming which demanded justification, verbalisation and conceptualisation.

My own self-image became, for some time, wrapped around the idea of what kind of artist I wished to become and what that could bring me. It was a shifting of identity to fit moulds of acceptability in a game of becoming and acquisition; even though we may not like the game, we can be drawn to the imagined prize at the end of the game, a conceptual image we have of the desirable that keeps our focus on 'end-gaining' rather than the here and now.

Yet the end of the game of becoming seemed to be an ever-moving feast, always just out of reach as the end time extended in a desire for that little bit more that was never quite enough.

On returning to college and city life I decided to live alone to give myself space to change and grow as needed. For I felt there were still so many patterns of fear, anger and guilt which constantly threatened to derail me. I was at war with what I did not want to feel and see; there were thoughts and feelings that were okay and others that were definitely not okay. The not okay ones simply had to go, by fair means or foul the unwanted had to go. My mental and emotional understanding at this time was very much based on eradication.

This was how I entered into shamanism. I felt I needed a good pruning and bandaging. Then I could be whole, normal and at ease with others and myself. I had no notions of befriending or welcoming anything I did not want. It was very telling that on the first workshop I planned to attend, as I drove there and approached the gate, I simply could not turn in. I just drove past as fear gripped me. I repeated this several times, each time not being able to turn in the gate. Deep down I knew that if I went in, I would be exposing myself and letting down my guard. That kind of naked vulnerability was truly terrifying.

I have since learned that fear itself, when faced, is a doorway to truth. Fear itself is a welcomed friend that stands on the threshold of our own home ground, like a siren to guide us. That orientation towards home is itself a magnetism, an irresistible pull to truth which lights the way, regardless of outer circumstances and, luckily for me that day, my steering wheel eventually turned and in I went, fear or no fear.

Shamanism was an unknown to me at that time and to some extent still is today, in that its core could be said to be mystery itself. At that time I had a vague notion that it was an ancient tradition of healing and interaction with the world that was indigenous to many lands—a world that was infused with Spirit, a Spirit that was in all of life—the trees, plants, animals and elements.

I found I had a natural affinity to the techniques of shamanism as a means to probe consciousness. Even in those first few introductory workshops there was a loosening of some of the bonds that held me in place. What became most obvious was how emotionally repressed I was. Any emotion throughout my life that had been judged to be negative, threatening, or unworthy had been pushed away, to be avoided at all costs. It felt as if there was an ocean of collected tears dammed behind my eyes, which blurred my vision and flooded my heart.

This introduction to my unhealthy pattern of aversion was revolutionary for me at the time. To feel into these patterns that were wound so tightly in the body-mind was remarkable. Combined with the insights that would come through the 'journey' work, it was very revealing. At this time I was more involved with facing and being with all that had been avoided, rather than probing the actual nature of aversion or the 'I' that avoided—this would come later.

For those not familiar with shamanic work, a journey is a means of exploring an altered state of consciousness, which is generally brought about by the use of a drum or rattle played at a continuous rhythm. One can journey with the intent, for example, to see a past event or trauma from a different perspective in order to gain new insight and release from a perceived problem. It can be a hugely creative and imaginative process of probing consciousness. This appealed to my artistic side, which loved the wonder of encountering guides, power animals and magical terrains.

This is not to say that it is a completely cerebral healing process, there is also a corresponding visceral component as the body processes and releases in a surprising number of ways. However, I was still very much of the mindset of division, there was a 'me' who needed healing, a separate little entity of a psychological self, which was embedded in and composed of oh so many layers of memories, beliefs and feelings. I believed that if I could just shed the unwanted layers, then 'I' would be just fine.

Nonetheless, I was very grateful for the insights and relief I felt at that time. I remember vividly my first shamanic journey where a few single tears rolled down my check as I was brought back to a half-forgotten time. A time when, as a child, I was handed a writhing bag of kittens and told to go down to the river and throw the bag in. I was bitten by parental authority, a fusion of love and fear that propelled me to an action that had not arisen from within. So on and on I ran to the river, a place I dearly loved as it held such mystery and beauty to a child's clear eyes. I had spent countless timeless days there playing and dreaming; there I was safe and free. As I ran, each footfall echoed the beat of fear that was growing in my heart as the thought of failure and disapproval spurred me on.

There, at the edge of innocence, I threw what was deemed unwanted into a place of magic, turning my back on discarded beauty in the name of approval that was fuelled by fear. The playing stopped here and life became that bit more serious.

In the journey I could feel the event with the same intensity as when it had initially happened, but this time I did not have to conceal anything. It was as if the energetic charge of that event had lodged as a holding pattern in my body, one informed by a child's view of the way the world was. This pattern, which had stayed unconscious, had no doubt coloured my subsequent view of the world. In the simple re-visiting and witnessing of the event and its charge, there was a release of tension that could be felt in the body as the loosening of a mental and emotional contraction. Those few simple tears that were shed may not seem like much, but when you have not shed a tear in over twenty years and your emotional body has been numbed in denial, it is like the first few drops of rain in the desert after a prolonged drought—you can feel that life is returning.

This was the beginning of a process that brought up much from the depths of the unconscious, revealing how events, people and conditions from the past had informed who I thought I was—not who I was, but who I thought I was. So often such conditionings give rise to unexamined, unconscious beliefs that form our identity, weaving core stories that reinforce behavioural patterns that perpetuate cycles of separation. Many people, at their core, believe themselves to be unworthy, bad, a victim, alone, unlovable. Upon revisiting such held memories in the light of truth, we can see that these memories are infused with beliefs. Yet beliefs are merely thoughts that we hold to be real and are based on a fragmented view of reality. A belief is never the truth—it is just a thought that we firmly identify with consciously or unconsciously. Often such beliefs are formed by a child's mind as a means to cope with and understand the world in which they find themselves. However, as an adult, if these hidden beliefs remain buried in the psyche, they are best re-examined as they can fuel behavioural patterns that no longer serve. Later, as the love of truth deepened, I would come to see that even the 'I' that believes must be questioned.

This early shamanic work was an exciting and challenging time of discovery. The time spent away from my life situation seemed like an oasis of calm wherein a deeper sense of self could be felt in safety. There was the learning of many new techniques such as stalking awareness, ancestor work, sweat lodges and spirit boats. These techniques brought about a shift in consciousness by altering the hold of consensus, waking consciousness.

I had experienced shifts in consciousness many times while making art, especially while sculpting. I would find myself slipping into a place of no thought, a present moment awareness outside of time. It could be likened to a flow of creativity that dissolved the subjective 'me-ness' in an effortless flow that allowed for spontaneous action to unfold in the silence of that flow, where the work took shape before my eyes. There was a great beauty and peace in the surrender to this flow and in the witnessing of the inherent creativity within.

So the altering of consciousness involved in shamanic techniques seemed a natural extension to the creativity I already felt in art. One such technique was 'stalking awareness,' in which one holds a question while out in nature, without using conceptual, rational intellect to formulate an answer, thereby letting nature and intuitive intelligence be the guide. In the non-engagement of the known, stillness becomes prominent. Nature then becomes like a mirror, reflecting back a clear and creative insight into the question held, without the usual thought processes involved.

I remember one such occasion as I sat by a tree, I held the intention for guidance on,

What is the next step to take?

The shamanic course I was on was coming to an end and it was not clear what way to proceed. Intuitive guidance can come in so many different ways, but for me it is often a soft, quiet voice, which is gentle and unassuming. This voice generally makes a short and simple suggestion without ever being repetitious or demanding, it also never argues or reasons things out. I find that it is only the internal voice of the egoic-mind that blusters, blames, argues, demands, debates and attempts to control. This gentle voice could be called the higher self, universal intelligence, or pure intuition, while the blustering voice of compulsive and comparative thinking could be called the egoic-mind.

  As I sat, I heard and felt the intuitive guidance to pick up a large stone, which was nearby. As I did this, I could see that under it were two large earthworms wrapped around each other, writhing and wriggling in an endless, spinning embrace. I was spellbound as I watched, at times it was hard to tell if it was one or two earthworms as the dance between them seemed to unify. This appearance of the two earthworms evoked the symbol of caduceus—two intertwining snakes with a winged top. As I watched on, a sense of reciprocity and balanced movement grew in stillness. There was something in the harmony of the two to be uncovered. This became more evident that evening as I glanced at a book with two interwoven serpents on the cover. I was immediately drawn to reading it. It was about a sacred plant medicine called *ayahuasca* from South America, a traditional medicine used for thousands of years to heal and guide. It seemed it had the capacity to aid in the release of deep traumas and addictions. I could immediately feel the pull, even without the knowledge of how or when.

Although I found the shamanic work of deep value, there was still a large schism between workshop Will and everyday Will. I felt I still had such deep, unseen and untouched drives within me that often propelled me against my better judgment and intention. I very rarely felt at peace or in harmony, just brief tantalising glimpses of presence which spoke of a deeper way of being. The confusion and divison I felt had been at play since I was a child and had rolled along into adolesence. In adolesence we often have an intuitive understanding that the roles people play and the roles that are being laid out ahead of us are not what we truly are. Here we sometimes try to break with the conventional, conditioned views of our family, culture, or society by entering sub, or counter-cultures. Yet the divison that we feel then in the world around us is but a reflection of the inner division that is at the core of our held identity.

At that transitory time of adolesence, I felt a distaste for trying to become any conventional role as a means to seek satisfaction. As, even then, I could see that people became hopelessly identified with their roles. Their sense of identity and self became derived from the job they had, or the position they held, or what they owned. These roles entailed attaining the job, the car, the partner, the house, the promotion and conforming to agreed-upon norms. This distaste resulted in a rejection of conformity on the surface layer. I lived for many years a hedonistic lifestyle of parties, drink, drugs, travel and mayhem, all the while trying to maximise pleasure by avoiding displeasure. I was firmly running the wheel of *samsara*, where craving and aversion were creating a momentum that did not allow for any stillness.

I had managed to come out of this lifestyle with only a few, more socially acceptable addicitons left—drinking and smoking. Yet addiction is addiction regardless of substance, whether it be cigarettes, shopping, fame, alcohol, money, prestige, cocaine, or sex. They are all deep patterns of searching for gratification and satisfaction in the outer world, a seeking to aquire that gives the feeling and sense of completeness. Yet this type of satisfaction never lasts for long and is always replaced with yet more desire.

I felt these patterns of momentum and becoming still move me. Even amidst the shamanic training I would find myself moved along in party scenes which had lost their flavour but not their allure. At the core of 'me' was the root addiction which was the momentum of becoming;

becoming whole and happy by getting what 'I' wanted and avoiding what 'I' did not want. On one such night I found myself past the city limits down at the docks, standing in the rain in a tee-shirt, silently screaming out to sea. I had no idea how I got there—there was just the longing to be home.

Plant sentience

I have found that discovering that which is already looking for you is grace itself wearing the mask of inevitability. With my curiosity aroused for ayahuasca I waited, openly holding that that which is dear to my heart will surely be. I did not, at the time, have the resources to travel to South America to find this healing medicine. An opportunity came nonetheless one weekend as I attended a shamanic gathering in Europe to celebrate the arrival of spring. Unbeknownst to me, there was an ayahuasquero there at the ceremony that had been invited to give a 'work' of ayahuasca after the weekend. A plant work is where one opens to the healing properties of a given plant, normally by ingesting it under the guidance of a skilled plant master. Over the couple of days I had noticed no special powers to this middle-aged man, except for the fact that he had very clear eyes and a calm presence which was not easily swayed by the games or machinations of those around.

I had been told who he was as we prepared a sweat lodge for that evening. As I sat across from him at the fire, I prayed internally for this sacred medicine to welcome me as I was and to help me to clear the patterns that bound me. Within a few minutes I was approached and asked if I would like to attend the ayahuasca ceremony the next night. My heart sang with the fullness of, 'Yes,' and my ears rang with the truth that what is for you will not pass you by. The sweat lodge that followed unfolded to a level I had never before felt, it was as if the medicine had somehow already started its work.

The sweat lodge began as normal but soon took on an intensity that shifted me into a new way of seeing. At one point, the lodge holder asked for someone to lead a chant. I found, to my surprise, that I had agreed to do it before I had even thought about it. This was strange, as I never talked much in circle, let alone sang—this was a big no-no. Yet as the rattling started I began to sing. It would be nice to say that my musical debut was astounding, but alas what came out of my mouth was the strangest, lowest, dirge-full mourning you could ever imagine. It seemed out of my control; it felt as if I was being sung, as if there was something deeper at play that needed voice and release.

I was but a channel for this energy of dense sorrow, grief and pain that was held in the land. Up it came, raised by the sweat, prayers and singing to be unblocked and released, drawn up in resonance with the collective intent of those who were present. As we worked, I witnessed the lodge light up with pinpoints of floating luminosities, as the trapped energy released. The sense of relief and peace became tangible in the lodge as we felt it draw to a close and out we crawled to a clear, star-studded sky. I fell back in the grass, wordless and watched as the trees that surrounded us lost their solidity and revealed themselves as self-luminous energy scintillating in salutation. Nature revealed itself as a river of effervescent awareness pulsating with the one light of being. Gradually, as I lay there earthing, my familiar sense of self came back and the seeing of unity was veiled once again by the reliable solidity of known objects.

I moved on to the next night and the meeting with ayahuasca with excitement and also a lot of apprehension. Fear so often arises when the mind is faced with an unknown—something that may be beyond its control. Yet at the same time there was a reassuring current of synchronicity, as if all was in hand and all was well. As we settled in, we were given some advice which I was to hear many times after and which served me well. The advice was that no matter what visions or feelings arose during the session, it was best not to turn from them; if you turned from them they would chase you, keeping you in a state of perpetual avoidance. Whatever happened, we were advised to stay with it and allow it to pass of its own accord. We were simply to let our breath guide our attention back to our heart whenever identification with thoughts was noticed. I came to see how important this advice was, not just for plant medicine work but also in the harmonisation process after awakening.

As the medicine took effect, I closed my eyes and lay back as I was engulfed by a vision of myself sinking down into the earth and being enveloped by a host of earthworms. The medicine was a key to consciousness wherein a world of inner visions and guidance was opened. I was shown areas in my life where doubt assailed me, how my pride held me from true communication and how my agendas stifled true spontaneity. On and on I was lovingly guided, as a mother would hold a cherished child, I was shown without judgement the areas where I blocked the flow of life. I began to see how all of these forms of control were a constriction—a resistance to life. In the seeing of these patterns there was no sense of overcoming them or changing them. The truth of clear seeing is, itself, the light of awareness, which is like a vanishing agent that leaves no untruth, hurt, or scar.

After a plant work one could feel tender energetically, psychologically, or physically, but there would also be a corresponding sense of relief and lightness. For days and weeks after each work one could feel an unfolding, as there was the opportunity to live and to embody what one had realised during the work. I found that old, reactive patterns were not so identified with and could be more easily witnessed as patterns of conditioned behaviour. Even if one became temporarily identified with a reactive pattern, there was always the chance of seeing it after the fact and this itself was a boon, as the hold or magnetism of these patterns began to fade. I found this medicine to truly be a medicine of the heart, if used wisely. It was my good fortune to have met an ayahuasquero who had integrity, honesty and a love for life.

I also noticed that working with this medicine brought one back to the position of the witness, a position I had become familiar with through meditation, where there was the clear recognition that one was not one's thoughts, sensations, or perceptions but the witnessing of all thoughts, sensations and perceptions. It was an interesting overlap and one I explored deeply much later.

In comparison to the gentle journey with the ayahuasca at the first work, I encountered another aspect of the medicine in the next work, which was uncompromisingly firm. During this work I was overcome by heaviness and negativity. I was assailed by images of war, brutality and obscenity that bubbled to the surface of my awareness with a very visceral feeling of pain and poisoning. Everything in me recoiled, I wanted to run far and fast, but where could I go to escape from what seemed to be inside of me? I was called to the altar for assistance. As the singing and rattling of the *shacapa* flowed, I felt my whole body clamp down like lock-down in a rioting prison: there would be no escape allowed.

I found myself gutturally growling through clenched teeth, paralysed with the fear of having been seen, like a wounded animal that had been cornered. As the intensity of the singing and rattling increased there was a corresponding inward contraction of resistance. Then, internally, I heard a voice say,

"I will kill him before I let him go."

These words seemed like they were the voice of the constricting, poisoning pain I felt inside—as if I was splintered within—and from the depths had arose a shadow of anger that was like a clenched ball of rage and control. To witness these words with the sheer anger and terror that went with them was, to say the least, shocking.

With that the singing and rattling came to an end and I lay back down as the tension in my body gradually lessened.

What on earth had I just witnessed?

This energy pattern did not feel like it had been released but simply flushed to the surface to be seen. I was asked many times that night if I needed help, but I refused. I was too confused as yet to fully go into it, my whole identity was rattling under the strain of division and there was neither the will nor the strength to fully explore it then. There seemed to be a deep divide within and I wondered was it a shadow aspect of the psyche or the voicing of the 'pain body,' as the accumulation of unprocessed hurts. Perhaps it was an entity, as, in the shamanic worldview, there are considered to be different energy forms that can attach to our energetic body in resonance, much like a parasite. I simply did not know.

Over the proceeding weeks, the sense of unease in me grew and I felt I could not wait until the next ayahuasca work, which was months away, to tackle this dilemma. During this time I had been reading some interesting accounts of medical testing with psilocybin for the relief of existential anxiety and depression in the terminally ill. Psilocybin has been traditionally used as a sacred healing and visionary medicine, particularly in Central America, where there is an unbroken tradition of its use among the indigenous population. Like ayahuasca, psilocybin acted like a key to consciousness, which allowed one to broaden limited perception and become sensitive to the filters of conditioning that often lie unexamined.

I'd had some experience with psilocybin in my youth, but then it was more taken out of a sense of fun and adventure. These explorations were sometimes not in the most conducive set or setting but nonetheless, it had proven to be a catalyst which had informed me of a different way of being, often bringing about moments of exquisite beauty. However, it was not obvious to me then how to engage it fully and work with it as a healing modality. Now though, there was a need and the way seemed open to explore such work.

So began my work with psilocybin semilanceata. It started initially with much trepidation, as I was not trained to work with it, nor did I know anyone who was. However, there was a strong guidance to work with this medicine and I found that I had a natural affinity with it. Many of the lessons I had learned with the ayahuasca, I now applied to this sacred medicine work, but it was the intelligence of the plant itself that was my teacher. It was a medicine that assisted me in facing and opening to the energy that had been raised at the previous ayahuasca work. Words fail to describe adequately the sense of anger, pain and turmoil that seemed to grip my entire system like a contracted, energetic spasm. The psilocybin helped to sensitise me to this energetic knot and to sit with it without aversion or denial. I began to fully feel into whatever presented itself and to allow the natural intelligence of presence to unwind all tensions in the sustained attention of acceptance. Like a breath that has been held for the longest time, these knots can become more intense just before the moment of release—the tensioning can seem to get tighter and more suffocating, but the absolute relief when the tension unwinds is a pure joy.

When someone has been in contraction for so long, it is only with a release that the extent of the tension that was held is known by the ease and sense of peace that comes to the fore. Much of the crippling sense of wrongness and self-consciousness that I had felt in daily life left with the release of this pattern and life took on a simplicity that I had not felt for many years. This, for me, was the real litmus test, in that the work done with the ayahuasca and psilocybin was making for happier and freer living. These plant works were harmonising inner and outer life by bringing consciousness to those areas that were unconscious, bringing light to what had been denied.

There were many plant works over the years, group ayahuasca works and solo explorations with psilocybin, both weaving together into the fabric of my life as an ever-deepening undoing of assumed identity. It was not always plain sailing however and the vagaries of human drama played out both inside and outside the works. I was not immune to such dramas, as my own egoic tendencies, pains and hurts rubbed up against 'the other' in the grit of life. Yet it is in the grit of life that our spiritual understanding is put to the test. In the furnace of relationship I found that what was petty, mean and impoverished in me was tempered in an egoic dance of attraction and aversion that began to find stillness in fusion.

Singing to the drums

Within a year of working with the plants, I came to a turning point. I had just finished my degree in Fine Art and all the while had been planning to continue on to do a masters or to work at becoming a gallery artist, with all that that entailed. I found however, that the taste for it was no longer palatable; it was a game I no longer had the will to play. The egoic dream of becoming an 'artistic somebody' could no longer be fed with the belief that it could bring me happiness.

For a time it became a no man's land. I did not know in which direction to step as creativity came to a standstill and along with this, I found myself in a not-soromantic relationship of nightmarish proportions that seemed to have a magnetic lock of inescapability. Looking back, I can see that it was a true gift in that it brought forth in me what was conditioned, base, controlling and fearful. A fierce grace was at work that did not let me avoid what was being held in the depths of shadow. The light of truth can be a fire that burns all resistance with a compassion that is uncompromising, allowing humility to bloom as the towering shade of pride takes a tumble.

An interesting point, at this stage, was a visit to a psychic to whom I gave no verbal direction or details. He went on to tell me how I was and had been attracting a certain kind of woman because of the hurts I held inside, but that this phase was just ending as I cleared what was held, making way for a different kind of relationship. Then, to my surprise, he told me that in the immediate future he could see me working with painting drums and rattles. I almost laughed when he said this because it seemed ludicrous, I still had notions and ideals of high art in white-boxed galleries with much ado, so this seemed beneath me as a career. Little did I know that drum and rattle work would become a great love and a magical adventure, which opened me to new possibilities of expanded perception, beauty and creativity that was all woven into a spirituality infused with the loving vibration of the plant spirit world.

He went on to tell me how my sensitivity to spirits and subtle layers was opening in a direction that would make itself clear if I took steps now and not in the future. As I took my leave, he handed me a book about plant spirit medicine as a gift. It is amazing to me how life is always in a flow of uncontrolled unfolding, yet most of the time, we try to control it with our ideas and beliefs of how the world should be, rather than just seeing and accepting how it actually is. Later too, I came to see how even visiting a psychic could be a form of avoidance, a means for 'me' to know that everything would be alright in the future. It was a way for the 'me' not to be present with whatever that moment was—a need to know that was a becoming in the outer world, but that could not tell me who I truly am. At best, a good psychic sees the karmic patterns of conditioning that unfold for the body-mind, but our essence is unconditioned and only to be found here and now.

The preceding year was a revelation for me in terms of plant medicine, which had deepened work by work to ever-subtler layers. As I sensitised to this way of working, I began to be able to see-feel subtle energy lines to a greater degree. What was most intriguing to me was to be able to see people 'lit up,' that is, I would see an energetic system of moving light woven into a person's physical body—rivers of beautiful intricate light. Within the system, to a greater or lesser degree, I would see 'knots' or blockages to the flow, which would affect the overall luminosity of the system.

This seeing developed as my own system cleared from long-held blockages. Blockages of beliefs and assumptions that were formed by long-past events that coloured and conditioned the way I thought of the world and how I saw the world. I started to realise that the statement 'seeing is believing' was not entirely accurate, it could be said that 'believing is seeing.' If a belief is probed it can be seen to be a thought or collection of thoughts, a pattern of thinking that informs 'me' both about myself and about a separate, outside world. Take, for example, I have a belief that the sky outside my window is blue, in a relative sense this is true and can be confirmed by another person who is looking out my window. Yet if there is just seeing without thinking, seeing in the absence of thoughts, then there is no blue, no sky and no window. Without any internal labelling as thoughts and words, there is no separate sky—it is indivisible from the hill, trees, birds, window, curtains and walls. In the silence of no thought there are no beliefs, just the totality that presents itself in the presence of that moment.

We hold so many beliefs to be true. However, no belief is ultimately true—truth is beyond all beliefs. It is not only the surface, conscious beliefs that colour our perception of the world, there are also unseen, unconscious beliefs that are the bedrock from where 'I' as a separate individual view the world. People often try to change their surface beliefs to have a better, more fulfilled life, but if their unconscious beliefs lie unexamined then there cannot be a true shift in perspective. Beliefs such as 'the world is dangerous' or 'I am abandoned' can be at the core of our story: our core belief. These beliefs also have corresponding feelings and emotions associated with them that are held as energetic patterns in the body that can become reactivated when triggered.

If, for example, we have a core story built upon the belief that the world is dangerous, when we encounter a new situation that may feel like an unknown, we may start to become anxious or fearful because, at the core, we feel that the world is not safe. The emotional charge of this will be reactivated, colouring our perception of the current situation and generating a conditioned response that is based on an old assumption that may lie unseen and unexamined. If you find yourself reacting to people or situations, again and again in the same inharmonious way, then you can be sure that there is an unconscious belief pattern at play.

I found the plant works to be a great means to explore these held beliefs and associated emotional patterns. The vibrational essence of the plants would flush up what was held, layer by layer, loosening the constricting patterns that limited the perceptual range of what was possible.

A turning point came for me one night as I worked with psilocybin. As I sat by my altar there came the soft voice of guidance that announced the presence of the ancestors. With that there entered three energy beings of such breathtaking beauty and fluidity, yet as they appeared I became gripped with fear. Not a fear of these beings themselves but a fear that came up as my belief structure rattled with the strain of holding up a defence against what was such a magnificent and beautiful mystery. The fear of the unknown is often what makes us grasp that bit tighter to our beliefs. I bowed my head as the sheer sight of these beings seemed to intensify the fear, but I recognised that the fear was in me and that there was no danger from them. I just said,

"Please help me to see through this fear."

No sooner had I said it than the beings merged into a tapestry of moving light that glided in and out of my body in a vibrational embrace. The transparent luminous beauty sang out that,

"There is nothing to fear."

These words were like a deep cleanse as it resounded throughout my being, touching the doubts and fears that acted like a shield of protection against the unknown.

It was then that I plunged ever deeper into the mystery of nature as the gateway to probe what was truly held within. I moved from the city to the countryside to be able to immerse myself in the rhythm of nature. I took a simple job washing dishes in a local restaurant in the evenings and I spent the days walking the hills and woods searching out flowers to make flower essences with. Each flower held a specific vibrational essence that was freely given upon request. The gratitude I felt towards these expressions of joy and creativity still resonates today.

As I learned to work with these disarmingly simple, subtle energies, I experienced a deeper letting go. Old patterns, memories and emotions would be flushed into conscious awareness to be faced from a new perspective of acceptance. I began to recognise that all of these repressed and denied patterns were really cherished guests that pointed to what bound 'me.' I was opening to the embrace of acceptance where there can be no other— just an effortless, unconditional love for all that is.

Nonetheless, at times it felt like a huge effort was needed as the work of the flower essences again and again undercut the conceptual framework of beliefs that held my very sense of separate self together. It so often felt like 'I' was dissolving beyond my control, for it was not always the ugly, unwanted beliefs that were explored, but also beliefs that I was quite attached to and did not want to let go of. At such moments, fear would arise as a self-defence mechanism, a contraction of 'no' that closed me off to the truth. However, the great beauty and medicine of the flower essences was that they would not force or condemn, their nature is the gentle flow of truth where one is free to engage and disengage. Yet their essence, much like their perfume, captivates the heart without an agenda, just a simple resonance that attracts like with like.

What really tested my ability to be open with these essences was when I began faintly to hear the inner voice of certain plants as a soft and gentle other-worldly song of their being. Often, I would fall asleep and dream of the spirit of a particular plant, which would guide me to resolve an issue from the past in the most creative way, as the fluidity of the dream world allowed for multiple perspectives.

One such dream came after working with a magic little forest flower called dog violet. In the dream there was the replaying of some old disagreements I had had with previous lovers. This time, however, I was witnessing it replaying from the perspective of the other person. In it I could see that I was not as completely right as I had thought myself to be. Feeling and seeing from the others' standpoint gave a more holistic view of all the patterns and misunderstandings involved. Where I had found 'them wrong' and 'me right' dissolved into a forgiveness that transcended such positions of right and wrong. I could see that there were patterns within patterns of conditioning on both sides of these old arguments and that to hold on to any position of rightness kept me in a state of separation and untouchability.

Shortly after this letting go, I came to be with my wife-to-be. It was a meeting in truth that sprang from a flower floating in the centre of a holy well at the site of Uisneach, the navel of Ireland. The marsh marigold flower let us begin to be together as we were, with an honesty and acceptance that drank deeply in the reflected love of our own very nature. The deepening of unconditioned love is an endless quench that is felt in space-time as a continual letting go of all that was and may be.

It was at this time I was asked to paint a drum, the first of many. It was for the ayahuasquero who had introduced me to the sacred heart medicine. I agreed, not knowing what it would entail, but happy to help, out of gratitude and respect. The design of the drum was straightforward until I came to the actual painting of the drum itself. I had just returned from a weeklong retreat, so I was as open and as sensitive as I had ever been. As I sat with the drum, I began to feel energetic currents course through my head and down my body. I found myself praying as I painted, a kind of spontaneous, wordless imaging of gratitude that infused the work. I had never before painted in this way. At times it would become so intense I would have to step away to cool down. Often this internal praying would come through as singing, an effortless release of pure sound that had a vibration much like the vibration of a flower essence.

This was not the first time this type of singing had come through, but it was the first time it had happened while painting. The first time it happened that I could clearly see it manifest was in a sweat lodge in which there was a particularly heavy energy that was stagnating and stifling the flow of the lodge and the people in it. My guidance was urging me to sing, but fear and the rationalising mind told me I did not know how to sing or what to sing. So I sat in silence, feeling the heaviness permeate the integrity of the lodge, but waiting for someone else to do something.

Then I started to see the heaviness in the lodge as a dark red, interlacing pattern of energy. With that I heard a soft innocent, childlike song come from me without my volition. The song was an expression of an uncaused inner joy that was fearless in its simplicity. As I sang I watched the song take shape as a golden, three-dimensional, moving mandala of intricate beauty. The song moved throughout the lodge dissolving the dark red pattern of heaviness and in its place there came a soothing sense of joy that lifted and helped others to find this joy as they joined in song.

All the while it felt as if 'I' was removed, just the witnessing of it unfolding, without having the sense of being the personal doer of it, yet my lips, tongue and lungs performed spontaneously. As the song came to an end I heard someone say,

"That was beautiful Will."

Hearing my name seemed to pull me back into myself and all I could say was,

"I was lost,"

That was what it truly felt like, that 'I' as a personal identity was not there; the singing arose in and of itself. Over the years I learned that this type of singing was a surrender of the personal me to the presence of the moment. I recognised that if a sense of doer-ship or ego crept into the singing, then it would lose its effortlessness, becoming forced and without true power or grace.

When I completed this first drum, I was blessed to be able to see it in action and it proved to be a great lesson. I watched as the ayahuasquero's singing and drumming radiated energetic lines around the room in the most exquisite patterns of light that touched and eased the held burdens of those there present—a beautiful expression of spirit that, at times, took on the form of an energetic eagle dipping and diving throughout the room. I was beginning to see the beauty of being at the subtle layers of vibration.

Over the years I was asked to paint more and more drums, eventually learning to make drums and rattles also. This work was magical and, in a way, was an energetic training that was both creative and challenging. Challenging in the sense that to be honest to the making and the singing of these drums, I had to let go more and more of personal control, to let what wanted to be, be. Often while working on custom drums I would get a real sense of how the drum was being infused with a particular energy to assist the person it was for, as each person could be going through any number of different phases—from a joyful celebration to a deep transitory period of shedding. While painting these drums I would sing to them, imprinting them with the song of surrender. Much like the way a flower can impart its essence to water to be later used in healing, the drum became the symbolic gateway to the presence of Spirit. The drum was an outer manifestation of an inner energy that became engaged and activated when drummed.

This work flowered and allowed me to step away from salaried work, which freed so much of my energy to delve ever deeper into what was unfolding. It was a gift I was truly grateful for.

At this time there were also two meetings with the embodied divine, which still reverberate and deepen today. The first was to be welcomed into the loving embrace of Mother Amma: Sri Mata Amritanandamayi. The first time I went to her *darshan* I was so self-conscious, feeling foolish to be kneeling in line in front of thousands of strangers to get a hug from a woman about whom I knew nothing. Oh so much melted away in that vast embrace and still does every time I get a chance to be in her presence. She found a place in my heart and on my altar straight away. I found that the photograph of her on the altar would act like a deep pool wherein I could sink back into the peace and love that welcomes all.

The other meeting was with Mother Meera, whose eyes struck in me a wordless remembrance. What that recognition was I couldn't say, words like 'infinite silence' and 'unfathomable mystery' can point towards it, but never adequately describe it. I felt an immediate devotion towards her and she has been a constant guide for me over the years. She has, time and time again, penetrated the layers of illusion that were so tightly bound to me that I could not see them. The fragrance of her being knew no boundary and shed light where it was most needed. This devotion became a love without longing in the surrender of self.

Once, as I sat before her image, I heard the clear gentle words,

"Everything I see is within me."

With these words I was overcome with a sense of connectedness that was a beauty beyond measure. I felt connected to the distant trees, the birds singing and a dog barking in the distance; I was one with all in the moment. This taste of oneness seemed to fade, much like it did when it was tasted the first time at the meditation retreat, yet the quality of it left a trace like an echo that was a reminder of a deeper nature. Time and time again the words, 'Everything I see is within me' would bubble to the surface over the years, enticing but totally baffling to the rational mind. I thought perhaps it was like a Zen koan, which is designed to take one beyond the conceptualising mind. Later I discovered that it was, in fact, pointing to a great spiritual truth.

Betwixt and between

The works with the plant medicines deepened over the years, bringing up layers of hidden drives, desire, fears and impulses, all the while hinting at a deeper, unified field of awareness; the substratum that could seem to have such an elusive quality. The plant works themselves blended into the rhythm of life and, as well as being a means to uncover internal blockages, they also had a great sense of fun, adventure and ease about them.

To start to loosen the narrow perceptual field that had blinkered one for so long was both exciting and challenging. Indeed, to see that perception of the world itself was malleable was a revelation and to understand that our view of the world is coloured by our held beliefs and thoughts prompted many questions as to the nature of Reality.

As I opened to this way, I began to learn to work with different plants, such as hawthorn and mapacho, through a process called *la dieta*, or 'the diet.' This method is part of the South American tradition of *vegetalismo* or *mestizo* shamanism. The diet consists of sensitising oneself by means of restricting one's intake of certain foods such as alcohol, sugar, dairy and meat for a period of time. It is often done in the isolation of a natural setting, to curtail the influence and distraction of the outside world. The aim of this sensitisation is to make oneself open and available for the spirit of the plant—its vibrational essence—to guide you. This can help in the healing process, much like working with flower essences in that each plant has specific qualities or attributes that can unblock certain patterns on an energetic level. Healers and shamans have noted these qualities over time and this information is often handed down from generation to generation in traditional indigenous societies. However, the qualities and spirit of the plant as guide is available to the sincere heart, regardless of tradition. Traditions can be valuable in helping to avoid certain dangers and pitfalls, but I learned that tradition could also come with its own mind-made idiosyncrasies and shadow aspects.

Day after day on the diet, one would attune to the frequency of the particular tree, plant, or vine that one worked with by ingesting its bark, berries, root, leaf, or flower. Often it would be the plant itself that would signal the best way to proceed. The vibrational frequency of the plant would resonate within one's own energetic and physical system, enabling one to see long-held patterns and memories with more clarity and understanding and allowing one to feel and come to terms with unresolved trauma or frozen emotions. The seclusion could be from a few days to a week or more in duration but the food restrictions could last from weeks to months afterwards, so that the body would be sensitive enough to allow the frequency of the plant to continue to unfold, sometimes culminating in the vibration of the plant taking root in one's system as the energy of an *icaro* or song. These songs become a way to call upon this vibrational energy when needed.

One of the clearest times I witnessed this happen was at a shamanic healing retreat in which there was a participant in deep distress. The man was contorting on the ground, locked in a pattern of fear and pain. The facilitator signalled for me to assist him with helping the man. As I lay my hand on his solar plexus, my hand and his solar plexus lit up into a mass of energetic strands and I could see the blockages pulsating under the strain of impeded flow. I watched as the teacher and I sang to him, the songs turning to visible energy lines that eased, soothed and untied what was arising in him as he became calm and peaceful in response. It was a valuable lesson in how the flow of clarity seeks to meet and ease that which is burdened and suffering.

I did many small plant diets of one or two days when I got the chance, just to start to get the feel for the energetic qualities of different plants. My first longer diet was for five days with the magical and beautiful hawthorn tree, a tree that always attracted me, from the scent of its flowers to the crimson display of its berries every autumn. It has long been known to be a tree of the heart and that is what called to me the most—to free the heart to love without conflict or division, embracing the immensity of life as it is.

It was a balm to be in seclusion and silence without the normal obligations and distractions for that time. Day by day, as I settled into the silent dialogue of inner exploration, the plant energy assisted in the emotional unfolding, as memories of long-forgotten incidents flowed to the surface. So many of these memories had associated feelings and subtle beliefs about what was my history, my story. There was a strange and beautiful alchemy at work, these old, forgotten memories and emotions were flushed to the surface where they could be fully felt and in the clear seeing of them there was a softening. A deeper understanding of it would come about from the gentle shift in perspective that the plant would engender, allowing for a transmutation through deep acceptance. What also became apparent was that these memories and emotions were energetic in nature, more of a moving vibrational pattern than a fixed form—patterns that had become slightly constricted from holding. I could also see how some of these unseen beliefs had helped to form some of my personal tendencies and behavioural traits over the years—patterns that had shaped my life and evidently not always so harmoniously.

It started to become clear to me that the identity I had of myself was shaped by so many unacknowledged forces, incidents and reactions. So much of what we take to be ourselves are but patterns within patterns formed and conditioned since childhood by unverified assumptions and beliefs that have been embedded and handed down by parents and society in the form of well-meaning control of what one should be and how one should be in the world.

One night, during the hawthorn diet, I awoke from sleep to the faint sounds of a woman singing in the most haunting tone, but for the life of me I could not pin point if it was internal or external. It was without locale but unmistakably present. I often found during the plant diets that the line between sleeping consciousness and waking consciousness would become blurred. The space of transition between the two would open up, revealing a pregnant void of possibility where the boundary between inner and outer identity held no sway. As the days passed, I noticed that the singing changed, it took on a quality that seemed ancient and strong with an intuitive, knowing intelligence that was neither bound nor owned.

The real value of the hawthorn diet however, was how it played out in relationships and day-to-day living in the days and weeks that followed it. This is where I started to notice a great shift in that I could see that I had lost a huge amount of self-consciousness, especially around groups of people. I had always had a feeling of being exposed, but this just vanished with the cleansing of the diet. There is a great magic in how, when something is truly seen without reaction, what was once a problem is freed. Without judgements and wrongness there is just the inseparable manifestation of life as it is.

In the weeks and months that followed, I would sometimes sit in silence with the hawthorn and sing my gratitude for all the help it had brought me. It was then that I had a very telling dream. During a plant diet it is often in dream consciousness that some of the teachings come. Free of many of the rigid belief structures of waking consciousness, here one's inner guidance can find a less constricted screen on which to paint an insight. In this dream, the spirit of the hawthorn came in the form of a woman who was singing the tenderest song of love that I had ever heard. The crystalline beauty of that song spoke, without language, of the purity of love without limits. As she sang, there were moments I became her and moments I became the song until there was no separation between us, just the singing of unconditional love from no-one to no-one, a limitless singing field of undivided joy.

A couple of days later, the current of this dream washed through into waking consciousness in an act of surrender. As I sat at my altar, I remembered words I had read earlier in the day by Mother Meera. She spoke of offering everything in your life up to the divine, regardless of content, which may be deemed by the mind to be good or bad. There is nothing that is distasteful to the divine and to simply offer everything to the divine is an act of selfless surrender. It is not important to judge yourself good or bad, as these are just relative terms that divide and limit. The importance is simply to surrender all to the divine, that nothing is withheld, avoided, or refused.

As I sat there gazing at her image, the words, 'Everything I see is within me,' resurfaced, but this time with a greater sense of immediacy than usual. An urgency gripped me with the inquiry,

"What is it to surrender?"

It was a term I was familiar with and had used on occasion, thinking I knew what it meant, but there and then I could truly see that I had never really got it. I had heard people speak of surrender and I had read about it in many spiritual books, yet it was elusive to me. There were times in the past when I had tried to surrender but, in truth, it had been surrendering as a means to acquire—a form of bargaining. It was the belief, which is only a thought, that if 'I' surrender then 'I' will get something in return, such as serenity, bliss, peace, or enlightenment. It was the play of mind, or psychological-self expecting to become bigger, better, shinier, holier. It was an effort for the sake of end-gaining. There had to be something in it for 'me.'

As I sat there, it felt like the admission of not-knowing 'what surrender was,' was in fact the mind realising that it could not penetrate this mystery. This not-knowing itself was really the beginning of the surrender of the mind—which is the known—to the mystery of the unknown. It was the admission of not-knowing that was a true step towards letting go of control. This not-knowing was like the sudden pull that a salmon in the depths of the ocean may feel when it turns to face its home spawning ground. This not-knowing was the opening to an inner return that is guided by an intuitive intelligence beyond the mind—it was the pull of the unknown.

This not-knowing was a surrender that stilled the mind, leaving it open to a deeper guidance that spoke as a direct, clear intuition. My gaze then shifted to a portrait of Ganesh, the remover of obstacles and I heard the words,

"What are you looking for?"

These words shook me as I could clearly see that what I had been looking for were mere mind images, ideas that I had had about wholeness, sacredness and God. Yet these thoughts were only constructs of the mind, concepts of divinity. What I was truly looking for was, in fact, unknown to me, for if I really knew what I was looking for, then I would not have to look for it, as I would already know it. You do not need to know what you already know. I had been trying to make known the unknown all along. As this was revealed, my body pulsed with energetic jolts and the room began to lose its concreteness as my head felt as if it was being cleaved in two.

That was when things got a little scary, to say the least. I started to feel the huge burden of waiting and the pain of holding the past as an identity, an identity that could not accept life exactly as it was. It was an identity of dissatisfaction with 'what is' that propelled it to seek salvation in an imagined future. A future state that always kept one at arm's length from the satisfaction of here and now—like a dog chasing its own tail, I had been in a spin of becoming that was an avoidance of being.

On and on I sank, as the crushing weight of existence got even heavier to bear. This little 'me' had been in a constant movement of becoming that knew no rest, I had always been trying to become something as a means to wholeness, yet it was based on a dissatisfaction that was the root of suffering. It was like I was being squeezed out of a separate sense of self, the movement of the seeker was being shown for what it was. But it was all I knew and I clung on for dear life. Flashing insights came of life emerging from the infinite void—planets, trees, flowers and universes arising and falling at that moment.

The immensity and pressure of it felt like it was crushing me to death—and all 'for what?' All the frustration of not-knowing 'why' arose in me as a defence against the unknown. 'I,' the thinker and questioner, rallied against the unknown, an unknown that threatened my very existence. The unknown factor of birth and death seemed to spiral around me in a dance of undoing. The non-acceptance of life was the individual who questioned,

"Why?"

A 'why' that sprung from the pain of isolation, a pain that was unbearable—the crushing weight of separation. Everything seemed to be screaming out at me to,

"Wake up, wake up,"

It was as if I was caught in some nightmare. There was nothing I could look at in the room that did not reflect back to me this call. Yet on and on I turned away, as if trying to save myself from annihilation. Layers and layers of me were being stripped away beyond comprehension, as if everything was unfolding in a single act of manifestation that was beyond my control. Then the mind threw up its last defence. Was I losing control? Images of madness were conjured up in an attempt to corral and contain the bastion of the known, but I was going beyond that now. There was no escape or hiding place, I was being torn between dread and awe. On and on I struggled to the last, as the patterns of resistance would neither allow for nor admit defeat, even as the very fabric of reality seemed to be calling out,

"Wake up, wake up."

I tried to stand to my feet but fell to my knees. I cried out in prayer and song for help, as I could bear no more. In that yielding there was a presence, which sang,

"Just accept, just accept."

I looked to the photo of Mother Meera once again where I could see a clear, golden energy radiate as the feeling overcame me to just surrender, accept, accept life as it is, here and now, as there is nothing to fear.

It was then that a giant energetic knot of 'No' was dissolved in the simple presence of a 'yes,' a yes to life exactly as it was, without control. All resistance faded as I said out loud,

"Yes."

I was brought to surrender by way of utter defeat, as how could I stand against what is? The sense of absolute relief I could never put into words, as all the pressure and anxiety left. Everything was deeply okay and there was nothing to worry about. I could see the simplicity of life as it is and the sense of peace that flowed from this realisation was bliss itself. All I could do was smile with joy.

The silent voice of Truth

From this deep seeing came an outpouring of joy—not a joy for any particular thing, but a joy which seemed to be an inherent aspect of surrender itself. With this letting go of control came an ease and a deep sense of peace. I found I could not bring myself to worry for the past or the future. The sheer delight in the simplicity of life as it is, without argument, with no feeling of should or shouldn't. There was just a deep acceptance that did not demand for anything that was not already present. At that time I couldn't exactly explain why this was, but that did not seem to matter. The living of surrender is a joy that is self-evident and self-confirming, a deep satisfaction without opposite or argument—a peace in being beyond rhyme or reason and I basked in it. It was akin to falling in love, where you lose yourself in the other, but this time the other is the entirety of life and you are not apart from it.

To be free in this way was almost childlike in nature, as there was just a flow of present-moment awareness without grasping, fearing, or worrying. The sense of relief could be compared to that sense of return to health after a long, hard, physical illness where vitality returns, not just to the physical body, but also to the emotional and mental faculties. The newness of each and every moment sang with a freshness that permeated each and every thing without reserve.

At times, I wondered was this it, was this the result of all the healing work and did I now not have to do any more? I did not know what would unfold, or if there were any further lessons needed, as everything felt so clear—I felt that I could not possibly be perturbed or lose this presence, as it was my true nature. I thought that if this were an awakening then it would be permanent, unshakable and unassailable. I can see now how I had certain beliefs and thoughts about what an awakening was and how it would be. The mind-made self is the consummate shape-shifter and has many ways to reweave itself; appropriation is the game it knows so well.

During that week there was such a beauty to this clear presence, but I also noticed a slight resistance to being around people whom I found difficult. I still held tightly to the view, however, that if 'I' was awakened then I was somehow untouchable. I could not see then that the egoic 'I' had reared another head, like a hungry, smiling hydra. As the week passed, anger towards someone flashed up into consciousness. It was an anger that was not acted upon, its arising and falling was witnessed. Yet a tiny, gnawing fear slipped in with the flavour of, 'oh no, I am losing it.'

The pull of the old, conditioned patterns of me were making an appearance and this did not sit with my belief about a bullet-proof awakening as something that would instantaneously make me immune to all old, conditioned patterns. I had yet to come across any teachings that referred to a process after awakening, only later did I come to see awakening in a different light.

As that week came to a close, I got into a situation where there was a misunderstanding in which I deemed another person to have insulted me. It was so strange to feel the rise of the defensive wave of indignation, judgement and recrimination wash over the clear and open awareness. This psychological armouring of 'me' seemed to veil that presence that knows no wrong. 'I' was back, identified as the wronged and for days my mind churned the incident over and over, like a cow chewing the cud to extract the maximum amount of nourishment to fuel its existence. The joy of being was veiled by a belief in 'me' as someone who needed protection from the opinions and actions of others. As the weeks passed, there was still an aftertaste of present-moment awareness, which echoed sweetly from time to time, but the sustenance of now appeared to be dimmed.

Within a month, I felt as if I was back, fully identified with the egoic, mind-made self. Yet this deep seeing had given a glimpse of a radiant being without limiting conditions that sang with a joy beyond measure. I knew now that there was natural state that was veiled by identification with thoughts and beliefs of a mind-made 'me,' but this veil had been proven to be, at the very least, moveable and perhaps dissolvable. I felt I just needed to keep working on the conditioned patterns of a separate me that obscured this natural state of being. I had for so long been engaged in clearing my patterns that there was still very much a sense of doer-ship that spun as a momentum, but this too would be seen in time. Later I came to see that nothing could truly hold back an ocean of unity, the taste of which becomes a resonance that permeates all in an embrace of welcoming and remembrance. Illusion can never be found or fought, as it has no independent reality. It is simply seen to have never been when one's perspective shifts from the limited me to a unity that is all—and nothing.

Though the lens of attention was back on the separate sense of self, there still came, over time, more and more gentle insights and reminders of our inherent, natural state. It was as if there was an undoing underway that was stripping away an undercurrent of held beliefs and assumptions. A spacious, energetic quality would overcome me at times with a vast calmness that radiated a sense that all was well, nothing was amiss and everything was deeply okay, even when, outwardly, things did not seem so. I found that the mantra, 'Everything I see is within me' seemed to coalesce into the feeling that arose within as a question,

"Who is life?"

I found this questioning strange, as life is not a person. I thought grammatically it would be correct to ask,

"What is life?"

But logical analysis would not sway this question. It was unyielding in its consistency and persistence. I would awaken each morning and it would be the first thing to come to mind, 'Who is life?' The urge would come so strongly throughout the day that the words, 'Who is life?' would simply roll off my tongue without my conscious volition and I would hear the words come from a depth that was beyond me. As much as my mind would wrestle with this question, I could not answer it, but on and on it went. As I did my chores around the house I would find myself singing, 'Who is life? Who is life?' The more the question came, the more intense the longing to know sang out.

Within a few weeks I went to Germany to visit Mother Meera. Day after day, as I sat in her silent presence I could see how the ego had co-opted the clear seeing of awakening as a new, improved identity. I could see how the mind had started to weave a story about 'my' awakening, actually practicing what it would say to others. It became so apparent how the egoic-mind tells stories to itself and others as a means to perpetuate its own existence. It looks for re-assurance of its own identity in the mirror of other. Yet the awakening itself had sung of a unity that needed no re-assurance from another; it was self-confirming and complete in itself.

The question, 'Who is life?' resounded like a primal drum beat that turned attention to a stillness beyond mind. The question itself was an unswerving desire for truth that was not within my personal control; what could I do but lay it at the feet of the Divine Mother as an act of devotion? My sense of personal will was shifting as I learned to surrender my sense of control and doer-ship in recognition that there is a greater will at work. I was beginning to see that even all that I offered up was already in the hands of the divine.

On the last night of darshan with Mother Meera, as I knelt in line, I prayed for help. It was a prayer that arose from the heart, wordlessly, silently and spontaneously. Its essence was a deepening into the unknown and was akin to a dam bursting its banks. The constricting walls of 'me' gave way to the water of life. The realisation began to dawn that this life is not 'my life,' that this sense of 'my' life was a fabrication bolstered by egoic-mind, a conditioned self that had me separated from the divine. It dawned on me that this life is 'God's Life,' that God is in all and is all, in every form, from a blade of grass to a mountain. If God is all, then all is one. My being had been singing out, 'Who is life?' and now a deeper truth was shown as I knelt before the Divine Mother,

"God is life!"

As she held my head in her hands I felt a sorrow release—the sorrow for the perceived separation that had seemed to keep me apart. But had we ever been truly apart? As I lifted my head, she looked into my eyes. I was being guided and welcomed home in the embrace of no other; a most beautiful dance between wisdom and devotion as each constantly yields to the other in the unifying truth beyond separation.

Nothing goes unseen

Outwardly, life moved in a gentler way as my perceptions of the world shifted in correlation to the dissolution of the perspective point of limited 'me.' So many of the constricting patterns that I had held were falling away. Patterns that had coloured the way the world was perceived, narrowing the view to fit my beliefs of how the world should be. As my limited sense of self diminished in clear seeing, I noticed that there was less argument within myself, with other people's behaviour and with the world at large. This was reflected in my life situation in which there was a greater sense of wonder and joy, but most of all, it was the beginning of a real sense of ease in being. Being itself had started to be seen as complete in itself and without any need of becoming anything.

As time passed, resistance to life's ups and downs faded, but not always with an effortless grace. Often old patterns would flare up and I would temporarily re-identify with an old thought form or emotional pattern, but even these could not be controlled—just simply witnessed, during or afterwards, without judgement.

Living and embodying a deep seeing or realisation is really where the truth of it finds expression and in so doing flushes up remaining patterns of untruth. These were not always easy to see, but I was learning that nothing could be avoided. Life became the ground wherein insights could flow into the daily affairs of bills, obligations, relationships and work. Here is where any remaining patterns of reactivity really showed their face. Old, entrenched core stories and beliefs that had been buried and obscured in the mists of time were uncovered, stories and beliefs whose duration lent them a seeming solidity that masked the truth of their impermanence.

It was with the assistance of the plant medicines that many of these remaining patterns were seen. One of the other plants that I worked with was mapacho, which is considered to be a sacred healing tobacco—not to be mistaken with the chemical-laden tobacco that is rolled out around the world in half-truths of greed. Many indigenous societies revered the sacred and curative properties of tobacco, considering it to have many beneficial energetic attributes and holding it to be a bridge between the seen and unseen. What I found and valued most about it was that it expressed a great ability to get to the truth, when used correctly. It was like an unstoppable steam train that cleared the way to the heart of a problem or issue.

The first time I experienced its power was at a workshop in Spain years before. The mapacho was macerated in water for several hours and the resulting infusion was then drank. This has a purgative effect, both physically and energetically, that works on deeply held patterns. It is also known to be able to clear long-held patterns of addiction, both physical and psychological. The night before I drank this medicine, I had a dream in which the spirit of the mapacho came to me and told me that it would help with my addictions. At the time I had been addicted to commercial cigarettes, a habit I had picked up while partying and had never been able to shake, despite many attempts of personal will power.

As I drank the mapacho liquid I felt it take effect immediately as a heat running throughout my body, along with an incredible sense of nausea. Then came a calmer period, which itself gave way to a feeling of cold constriction. I would get flashes of memories along with very visceral body sensations as the mapacho flushed through the body. It seemed to pull related tensions and unease to the stomach and solar plexus area where the feeling of incredible nausea would crescendo.

This first time I worked with it, I fought it to the bitter end. I found it so uncompromisingly forceful, yet I resisted letting go. No matter how much we think we want to clear an addictive pattern, there is still the pattern itself, which could be likened to energetic tendrils or filaments that are wound within our body-mind system.

These patterns are sentient to a degree, in that the pattern itself seeks it own continuation or existence. These patterns or knots get sustenance from attention, or energy we give them through the form of thoughts, emotions and sensations. We can find these pleasurable and a desire can arise for more, giving more strength to the addiction. The thoughts or sensations that we find desirable can be elicited by many different stimulants such as money, sex, drugs, or alcohol, which give a temporary high, calmness, or pleasure but as it is temporary, it soon wears off leaving us craving more and here is where an addiction can take hold. An addiction can be subtle or obvious and can come in the guise of a few glasses of wine that help us to forget the day's woes, to the business deal that may bring us the big bonus, to the addict on the street who is desperate for the next fix. To a greater or lesser degree, many of us have physical, emotional, or psychological addictions, addictions that are wound in and around our sense of self, with the result that often these addictions come to define us, becoming who we think we are.

On drinking that first mapacho I knew it as a means of clear seeing. It is in fully seeing a pattern and its source that it is dissolved. Clear seeing involves more than inner sight, it is a knowing feeling that comes fully formed and is self-confirming. It is a clarity that can penetrate the shadows, where so many of our patterns can get pushed to in the polishing of our persona. The addiction feeds the imagined persona as much as it does the shadow. The two are not mutually exclusive but are interrelated opposites —one opposite cannot be without its corresponding other.

So, even with this resistance to the medicine of the mapacho, there was still a ripeness to see the truth which, combined with the vibrational quality of the mapacho, brought about a deep purge and a release of the pattern of addiction. It was not pleasant in the moment but hugely relieving and with the result that I could not bring myself to smoke commercial cigarettes again. No personal will power was needed to stop smoking, just the release that came in the clear seeing that transmuted the pattern of addiction.

That was the start of my work with mapacho, which deepened over the years. I began to see and understand that the work with mapacho was not just good for substance addictions, but also worked well with emotional and psychological patterns with which we have become deeply identified. Whether we are addicted to alcohol, money, sex, control, pain, grief, violence, prestige, hate, pity, victim hood, opinions, religion, or politics, it all comes down to the simple fact that we believe in them and want them because they enhance our sense of self. We believe these patterns help to define ourselves as the person we want to be, consciously or unconsciously. These patterns are the structuring of the separate self.

Often, as I worked with the plants, I would see these patterns as energetic filaments knotted in the body—patterns related to conditioning, beliefs and trauma. I noticed how these patterns vibrated at a frequency that tended to attract people or situations in life that would reinforce those same patterns. It was as if life reflected back to us what we held and believed inside. I was beginning to see that what is seen is a projection of the mind. I could see it played out in life, where the same addictive patterns were repeated again and again. People could get caught in the same type of relationships or hurts, time and time again, as if they were in a playback loop. The same was true for me, but as I became aware of many of my own patterns I found that life was free to flow in new directions.

I came to see that many such held patterns could be soothed and teased free with the vibrational assistance of the plant medicines. I would often sit with an essence or a plant that had drawn my attention to it, attuning to its vibration as a means to clear seeing.

One such evening as I worked, I found my attention drawn to an energetic knot in my calf muscle that was related to an injury I had sustained many years before that I could not fully recall. Regardless of the time that had passed, there still seemed to be an old charge held there. As I let my attention go to it, it felt like I became locked in a holding pattern of anger and frustration. I could see energy lines contracted into a ball in the calf muscle and whatever I did seemed to tie me to it even further, until it became like a battle of dominion. I wanted rid of it as the frustration mounted, then, just as it came to a crux, I looked to the photo of Mother Meera and heard the words,

"Even the knots are God!"

With these words I softened and no longer fought the pattern in an effort to remove it or change it—how could I fight God? This pattern was, in essence, divine and no other. When this was seen, the full memory of the injury came back. I had been in a school 200m running race and as we turned the corner, I was neck and neck with another student for a medal. I could feel he had me beaten. In the moment I could not accept this, so I subtly tripped him, knocking him out of the race to get the medal in the eyes of others. I had cheated to avoid defeat and to be a winner and in the process I had hurt my calf muscle and imprinted the belief that it was okay to dominate others to get what I wanted. I had pushed the full memory of this aside, but the energy body records all and is a vibrational storehouse where nothing can go astray. Once this pattern ceased to be avoided or fought it had the chance to be clearly seen and the underlying belief could be freshly tested for its validity. When a belief is seen we need only ask, 'is this really true?' In that questioning any untruth gives way and no longer holds sway. I wonder how many times this unconscious belief had influenced decisions in my life since then…

Over the years I came to see subtler and subtler patterns of beliefs that were half-hidden, yet all interlacing to form a worldview that had shaped 'my' life. Probing such conditioning requires a devotion to truth above all else, as each pattern emerges to the light of awareness in an unveiling that is really the unfolding of the psychological self.

My work with the mapacho grew in time, as I learned to carry a pipe and diet with the plant. On one such diet, I sat with the mapacho for seven days in silence and solitude as I learned to connect with its clearing vibration. During this diet I came to re-taste the spacious awareness that is never tarnished by the ebb and flow of thoughts and emotions.

It was only when I got the chance to travel to Iquitos in Peru, to diet with a mapacho master, that I got to see the living tradition of *curanderismo* in action in a society in which it is woven into the psyche and beliefs of over a quarter of the population.

My intent for this diet was for a deep clearing of all attachments to fears, pains from the past and worries for the future. This intent stemmed from my life situation at the time where old patterns of buried fear had arisen around security. This then had become reflected in life as a continued trespassing of our land, which ignited in me such feelings of threat, violence and reprisal in a fog of mental noise: a mental stirring that argued against what was with the voice of blame, injustice and judgement that had the tone of so many repressed, unforgiven altercations from the past.

It was plain to see that these memories of the past, which are only thoughts, had a corresponding emotional imprint and charge that would elicit another thought pattern, fuelling a never-ending cycle of thoughts and emotions; a tenacious spinning circle of emotions and memories that seemed to define my story and had a gravitational pull that could keep one identified with an agitated state of confusion and pain. It was the movement of egoic-mind as a collection of thoughts and emotions that spun around so fast, from one to the other, that gave the impression of solidity—a contracted body of offence and defence.

There was no hiding out in previous, comfortable realisations of 'there is only life as it is,' because this was life and it had flushed up a hornet's nest of hidden ill will and fears. The flow of life, that did not recognise any holding or separation, had brought me a deeper gift, if I just had the wherewithal to see. For hiding out entails the hiding from, a game of cat and mouse duality that relies on the positions of 'me' and 'other,' of 'right' and 'wrong,' of 'good' and 'bad.' The jig was up, yet the dancers still spun—albeit in ever decreasing circles.

This mapacho diet tackled long-held ancestral patterns of pain and violence that had echoed down my lineage. Night after night as we worked, we would sit in the dark as the mapacho master sang his songs of light that beckoned all shadows home to their transparency. During each work I would see and be able to track past pains that had moved from parent to child for generations. These very inherited knots could further entangle one in deeper personal *karma* in the continuance of cause and effect, but they could also be the means of transcendence. For why we are born to any particular family is no accident. These very familial conditions are the composite of life that can help one to outgrow the belief in any limiting conditioning.

One day blurred into the next as pattern after pattern was seen, so many tangled knots that seemed to claim me as their property. Memories of childhood tears of loss enmeshed in adolescent grief and blame, tied together with adult half-truths, lies and shame. All calling me by name,

"You are Will and we are you!"

Yet the master's song would light the room in tones of unrelenting release, a warm wave of voice washing over a frozen past. Night after night surges of expansion would weave through both waking and dreaming states as the body-mind purged and surrendered its confession of 'not me,' stripping me of my armour of judgments and self-judgements in an act of fierce mercy among the snot, the puke and the tears.

The force of this diet came crashing through in a very real way when I got back to Ireland. Within hours of arriving home, I came face to face with an angry man wielding a hammer who was trying to knock down our gate. Life was immediately offering me the possibility of acting from the moment, free of reactivity fuelled by fear and violence from the past. As I walked towards that man, unarmed of the past, I was really moving beyond fear of the unknown with every step. I had no idea what I would do or say but what transpired was the beginning of the resolution of the other as enemy; I was beginning to see no other in the eyes of all. Without personal premeditation, there is seen to be a spontaneous functioning to every moment that is uniquely creative. A functioning that is beyond control and is a freedom beyond the known. While that functioning, at another time, may have had me simply walk away, each moment elicits its own response that is free to be when we are not re-acting from unconscious conditioning.

Retiring from imagined control

Over time, the work with the mapacho deepened alongside the work with other healing plants. Blending ever more seamlessly into a life that is not separate from spirituality, but a life that encompasses both spiritual and secular with ease. There is a great beauty in the flow of life that cannot be held or divided. Even the seeming knots of life are the totality singing an unconditional love song of deep acceptance.

As I sat at my altar one night smoking my pipe, I started to feel the culmination of a deep questioning. For many years I had been working with the plants in a process of untying the strands of constriction that had caused so much confusion, pain and suffering. I had reached a point in my life where I was relatively happy and not burdened by the woes of past regrets. There was a sense of ease and peace about myself that was true gift in itself, yet there was still a sense of 'not quite there yet.'

Out of all this work, what seemed to be appearing was the path of a plant healer. Certain skills and energetic abilities where coming to the fore indicating that perhaps I may be able to work with the plants in a capacity to guide other people, especially as I had worked through so many of my own conditionings—the path of the wounded healer, as it is often called. Yet my guidance was always just to keep going, clearing and seeing ever deeper. There was a primal fascination with what was the core or truth of all this interaction with the plants and healing essences. This fascination was a pull that often kept me going, even when egoic-mind would caution otherwise. In a way, it could be called a drive or love of Truth itself, Truth for the sake of Truth and, as I sat that night, I felt its pull ever stronger, forming as a razor sharp questioning that was ready to cut to the core.

It had been churning around in me for some time as to my exact relationship to the plants and in particular to mapacho. So I sat at our altar and simply voiced my question,

"What is my relationship to mapacho?"

There was a deep yearning to know if I was to work and serve with this plant. I asked with an earnestness that just wishes to see the truth of it, regardless of the outcome—an unbending intent to see clearly. I petitioned the spirit of the mapacho itself to reveal the truth of our relationship. In the past it had, many times, shown its energetic strength and favour—yet there was no answer forthcoming.

The more there was no answer, the more persistently I held to this longing for clarity. I looked to the photo of Mother Meera and remembered her recommendation, which was to ask *Paramatman* directly, Paramatman being a term used to denote the Supreme Self or Spirit.

I asked as directly as I knew how,

"Please help me Paramatman."

It was asked as a child would ask, with sincerity to know the truth, regardless of outcome or appearance. I saw the plant healing work as a path of service to the divine and, if I was to walk this path, then I sought the direct guidance and approval of the divine. I held the question firm to my heart as I sat smoking mapacho, deeply inhaling and welcoming in the spirit of this plant that had washed through many of my addictive patterns and held beliefs.

Then the answer came, but not in a way I could ever have imagined. All of a sudden it was as if I was turned inside out energetically as I heard the words,

"Who is the 'I' that is asking?"

The table had been turned, I had been questioning my relationship to the plants and now 'I' was under question. The question had turned in on itself revealing a deeper inquiry,

"Who am I?"

The questioner was under question!

As this turning happened, I fell back from my sitting position onto my back as the very reality of 'me' was being probed. A feeling of terror ran through my body as if I was gripped in a death spasm. I witnessed 'my mind,' which was in a panicked state, trying to protect its identity from annihilation, as my body shook and convulsed. All the while this sense of witnessing grew in distance from the body-mind. At times I would be calmly witnessing it all unfold and at other times attention would identify with the body-mind pattern of 'me,' which was desperately fighting and resisting. I was alternating from witnessing the terror to being the terror. This very sense of 'me' felt like a ball of resistance that just could not let go as I oscillated between perspectives.

Then it all stopped as quickly as it had come over me. I was released from this death grip and all was as it had been, except, as I lay there, I knew that a deep fear and rage held this sense of 'me' together. I had witnessed it from a perspective of detached calm that was untouched. With this event came a feeling of loosening but not of release. I had gone as far as I could this time and no more. I came to see that the first big seeing that I had had, where I had said 'yes' to life, was a release of a deep resistance—a mental frustration and refusal that was a fixation point for the little 'me.' Along with this was the seeing that, 'God is Life,' a taste of unity consciousness. Yet somehow the sense of separate 'me' had continued as a knot of resistance that held its cohesion with a defence of fear and rage.

This event heralded the start of a very intense period of self-inquiry. What started to come out of it was a deep feeling for the need to retire. Retire from what and to where I did not know, but nonetheless this feeling gained in intensity week-by-week, month-by-month to the degree that the feeling became like an energetic vice that overcame me to the point of collapse. A sense of heaviness, confusion and constriction came to the fore as I pondered the fear and clinging terror I had encountered. The split between the witnessing of the body-mind and identification with body-mind had brought about an awareness that seemed to intensify the sense of resistance. Was I this aware, witnessing presence or the struggling, fearful body-mind? My attention had moved between the two as I had been gripped that night in a death spasm.

It started to become apparent that the body-mind identity, which I took myself to be, both consciously and unconsciously, was itself a pattern. I had worked with the plants to undo so many of my patterns of behaviour—addiction, grief and depression. Now I was being presented with the possibility that my very sense of individuality, of being a separate self, was in fact an energetic pattern in itself: a knot of resistance of limited identification. More and more I questioned the validity of this separate sense of self, its nature and source.

Over the years there had been the stripping away of so many of the heavy layers of identity, now it seemed the challenge was to engage the root of identity itself. I realised there must have been many others who had come to this point of engagement, yet I found no real depth of information on it in the shamanic literature that I came across. It was not until my search encompassed a broader range that I found a resonance of deep truth in the form of Ramana Maharshi. As soon as I saw his image I knew there was clarity and truth in form. His teaching spoke of coming to Reality by seeing what was unreal by means of self-inquiry, which entailed turning the mind to the question,

"Who am I?"

This questioning brought constant attention to the inner awareness of 'I am,' which then threw light onto the unreality of the personal 'I' thought. When the mind was turned back in on itself with the question, 'Who am I?' then it would meet the silence of the unknown and there would be an awakening to the natural, open, permanent state.

This echoed what I had come to experience and was a confirmation to keep working with self-inquiry. What struck me the most was his suggestion that the separate identity was but a thought and that this would reveal itself when the 'I' was tracked to its source. This tracking redirected attention from the mind, which is always in movement towards objects, back in on itself, leaving attention on the subjective 'I.' This, he said, would lead one to a direct realisation of the Ultimate Self and this Truth was the end of all questioning and searching.

I had come to see that there still seemed, very much, to be a separate 'me' that was very fearful for its survival, a 'me' of body and mind, made from so many emotions, beliefs, thoughts and memories. Yet in the death spasm, I had witnessed the body-mind pattern and if 'I' could witness this body-mind pattern, then it was an object that the subjective 'I' could perceive. 'I' was not the object being witnessed, but the subjective 'I' that was witnessing. What or who was this subjective 'I'?

At this time, in daily life, I was very busy with the work of self-building our own little home and there was very little time, if any, for sitting meditation. Nonetheless self-inquiry itself was woven into the work each day. While hammering, sawing, or lifting, the questioning feeling, 'Who am I?' would bubble to the surface. Often it would arise with such force that I would have to put down my work tools as it washed over me. I would take a breath and then go back to work. The inquiry had a pace of its own that was not repetitive or strained, but sprang from a deep source of calling—the irresistible pull of Truth. It rang with a freshness that did not engage the mind with philosophising or analysing—like boring a well, where only the sight of water confirms its source and presence. On and on the questioning went, to an ever-spiralling depth, in a longing to quench a thirst.

At the same time there was a deep question around the whole notion of protection. This sense of 'me' always seemed to be in a constant stance of protection, a fortification against a hostile outer world. This was also echoed in the shamanic worldview where protection was paramount, in that one had to establish good relations with the energies and spirits with whom one worked and also establish boundaries to keep out disruptive or harmful spirits. There was also the potential need for protection from other shamans who may have mal-intent towards you, or your work. In many indigenous societies that still practise shamanism, there can be energetic warfare between rival shamans, often representing their respective communities or clients, in which energetic vibrations are used to cause illness or harm. These vibrations are called darts in some traditions and have a dual nature—they can be used to protect or to attack. These darts are energetic patterns moulded by the intent of the shaman in co-operation with different elemental energies. Just as healing plant songs I had been given could help to untie the patterns of hurt in the energy body, so too could these darts be sung with the intent to cause harm or to curse.

In the plant tradition of curanderismo of South America this is often played out in an energetic warfare between forces deemed to be good and bad, light and dark, with the threat of attack or retaliation imminent. Many healers there spend a lot of time dieting with the plants to learn the energetic vibrations of healing and clearing but also of defending and attacking. A dark shaman is sometimes referred to as a *brujo*, one who works for personal gain for themselves, or their client and is not averse to taking whatever means necessary to achieve the sought-for result. This may sound like a reproach on this healing modality but it is really just an egoic, human characteristic, a mindset that can be seen in so many facets of life—from a solicitor who will do anything to get the job done, a police officer who will bend the rules, a businessperson who will crush an opponent, to an athlete who will do what he or she must to win the race. It is a matter of degree as to how far one will go to achieve the desired result. It is all based on a separate individual or a group of individuals seeking to gain a result: end-gaining. It is a very human, egoic characteristic of the 'me' getting what it deems desirable, whether it is money, revenge, power, or glory.

As I learned to work with the plants, I began to see such energetic vibration as flows of energy and intent. It was a process in which I also began to see where there lay hidden desires within me. Years before this, as I worked one night, I could see a sea of the most beautiful, intricate, energetic, moving vibrations coil around my body; it was the embrace of the energetic signature of psilocybin. It was becoming my ally, a guide and entry point to expanded states of consciousness where I began to see into subtler vibratory layers and other energetic realms. Later I came to see that all altered states come and go and are but an appearance in the true, open, natural state, which is permanent and unchanging. I felt it to be such a gift to be given the chance to learn in this way—to move through conditioned perceptual boundaries was a challenge and a joy. I sat in awe of this energetic seeing, marvelling at this display of consciousness. I could feel and see this signature of light respond and move to my intent and mood. In that expanded state, time and space were of a different quality—seeing and action were not restrained by agreed, collective cohesion.

Then, in the blink of an eye, these beautiful flowing patterns of light coalesced and transformed into snake-like arrows with teeth and menace, like a shoal of fish instantaneously and collectively turning to respond to a threat in the environment. In that split second they morphed and started to move from me with great speed. What I barely detected was that I had had a very subtle, low-level memory of someone from my past that I deemed to have hurt me. In that memory was embedded anger and resentment towards that person and that's where these arrows were headed—seeking their target in response to my belief. As they moved I just managed to shout,

"Stop!"

With that, they came back and circled around me once again in their beautiful form. I said inwardly to the plant essence,

"I will not work with you if you are like this"

In the gentlest response, I heard,

"It is not us who is like this."

With this I clearly saw that the psilocybin consciousness itself was neutral and that it simply responded to the intent of the person with whom it had merged. It was 'me,' with my unseen, held poison of anger and resentment that was the polluting factor.

I could see the huge potential for healing with the plants and also the inherent danger. For it is what we, as humans, bring to it that is the deciding factor. Our own dual conditioning colours the interaction. I could see how my own lack of clarity or unconsciousness could corrupt what was essentially neither good nor bad. I then bowed my head and asked the help of the plant essence to clear me of this pattern of resentment, so that I could work with it as clearly as possible. With that the patterns of light turned and went within me, unbinding me from the hold of unseen beliefs, memories and thoughts. For years I worked with many of the plants in this way, uncovering layer after layer of conditioning. It was vital while working with the plants to be aware of one's thoughts and emotions—otherwise one would emit a vibration that was energetically polluting. I would like to say that I was flawless in my work, but I was not. Sometimes, I was taken over by my own pride and arrogance in an egoic stance of self-righteousness that would cloud true seeing and healing.

I spoke with one plant master about this subject and I put it to him that, in essence, anyone who is identified with the egoic-mind is a brujo, as it is the ego that manipulates to get what it wants. To this he agreed, but added that it was not the case if you were in control of the ego, having one's ego on a 'tight leash.' It would seem that, in order to become a plant master, one had to control one's ego constantly for fear of being a brujo. For many years I had seen the rationale of this but gradually, it dawned on me, exactly who is the one holding the leash?

Who is the one controlling the ego?

Is it not simply the ego in another guise? The belief of being a separate individual in control is the structuring of egoic-mind. Only the ego would try to control the ego, giving credence to the illusory, separate self. It all boiled back down to the question,

"Who or what am I?"

People often refer to 'the middle way' as if it is a narrow path through polar opposites, a squeeze between 'good and bad' where constant vigilance, control and effort are needed for fear of falling by the wayside. But who is the one controlling? Perhaps 'the middle way' can be better understood as the encompassing of 'good and bad,' where they are not seen as diametrically opposed, but rather as interrelated variables within a continuum in which the holding of one side is seen to bolster the other; any idea of 'bad' can only exist with the holding of what is deemed 'good.' Holding one side maintains the other as separate. Investigation into this controlling and judging 'I' is the move to transcend all opposites, even the notions of 'spirit and matter' may eventually be seen to be undifferentiated.

No self, no other

This period of self-inquiry built in intensity to a staggering degree in the months leading up to my fortieth birthday. Along with the physical exhaustion of building our home was felt the inward pull to Truth. Every movement and thought seemed to be marred by a viscosity, as if I was moving within a world of thick treacle, where every step was like a struggle against an outer force that threatened to crush me. My mood became heavy, which matched my physical and mental torpor. Ever increasing was this feeling for the need to retire. A feeling that was like a constant drone of,

"Enough."

Yet on I ploughed as the mind could see no way out—it simply had no idea what was to be stepped out of, or how. The struggle I felt so deeply I could see reflected in the compassion and concern in my wife's eyes. For all the constriction I was feeling, she, no doubt, felt the pangs of one who deeply cared, yet knew it was beyond all control, for what was shifting would take its own course.

For my birthday we spent the day visiting some ancient Celtic sites. First we went to Kesh caves, reputed to be the entrance to the underworld in Celtic lore, a place of beauty and magic. It eased my heart to climb those gentle, sacred slopes. We explored the different caves, both together and alone, finding a moist, rich, silence punctuated by the gentle trickle of water that soaked down through the mountain, dropping from roof to pool in a natural, simple symphony. I moved through one small cave that narrowed to such a degree that moving sideways, I had to inhale to squeeze through. Being held in that tight cave was a constriction of sorts, but one that could be tangibly seen and felt as cold hard rock. I rested there as the rock held my body in place, relieved not to have to support myself. There, as I rested, my mind quietened and my sight was drawn down the length of the cave to the small gap of open sky and light. Held there, in this earthen womb, a singing prayer arose within, a soft whisper that echoed out to the light. I felt the pang of 'enough,' cradled in the ancient sedimentary care of unfolding, all was moving to an unseen rhythm. I could see that the constricting contractions I had been going through where the natural precursor to a release, the pulse of life that birthed ever anew into an ever-flowing expanse without end; a dying and birthing of wings without flock or feather.

Later, we continued on to Knocknarea Mountain, an ancient site with a strong history and a majestic energy. The first time I had climbed it, ten years before, I had been gifted with a taste of such expanse and ease. As I lay in the heather at the top of the mountain, my mind had shut down, a moment of no 'me' that had resounded through the years as a hint of the timeless, unbroken state beyond the 'I' of the mind, a calling home to what had always been. This time, as I climbed up and down those slopes, all I felt was a sense of the end of outer movement. I felt that what was calling me was not to be found outside myself, in any outer object, place or person. It was somewhat shocking to see that nothing outside of myself was ever going to satisfy me. It was a dying to the outside world of other and a feeling of crushing defeat.

This sense of losing the outer stayed with me throughout that evening and into the next day. As I sat at my altar, a deep silence overcame me. In it was no urge to probe or to clear, there was no more to be done as the question, 'Who am I?' had gone to a depth beyond volition. As I looked upon the photographic faces on the altar: Mother Amma, Ramana, Mother Meera and Genesh, I was without a clue how to proceed. It was not lost on me the fact that these photographic representations were all of Indian descent and yet here I was, steeped in a South American-Celtic plant teaching. All these faces reflected a tradition that spoke of self-realisation beyond all tradition: the Ultimate Truth or Supreme Self. I looked to these reproduced photographic eyes of Avatar, God and Sat Guru in wonderment. What connected me, my self, to all these 'eyes' or 'I's? So often in the past I had looked to them as guides with a willingness to learn and grow, a petition of becoming. Now, the 'I' who sought was silenced by an inward turning question, 'Who am I?' and I simply had no answer.

Those three years earlier, when I had asked Mother Meera about the nature of surrender, I had been given a taste of unity consciousness that was still felt as an undercurrent of being. Yet there was still, very much, an identity of separate 'me' or 'self' to the foreground. A 'self' or 'me' that at times seemed to veil the truth of unity.

As I sat, a ripple of energy moved through my body and my hands started to move in a flow of untying gestures around the body, as if they were subtly undoing energetic strands of identity—past tendencies formed as patterns. My hands moved without personal effort in a dynamic flow. Then my left hand went out, with palm outstretched in supplication to the photo of Mother Meera. I heard the words come from my mouth,

"I am ready."

With that, a shuddering energy ran throughout the body, knocking the breath from its natural rhythm. The altar and room took on a luminescence; everything was alight with waves of peace and bliss. The joy of being was self-evident and the intoxication of it was sweeping me away in the unity of life. It was as it had been three years before, how could I have forgotten the clarity of this truth? An outpouring of gratitude welled up, all I wanted to do was rejoice and be swept along in the bliss of it.

Yet as I looked to the photo of Mother Meera, the gentle voice of guidance whispered,

"Dare to look further."

As I focused my attention on these words and her eyes, the stillness deepened. The beauty of this unity consciousness was embracing all as divine and I could see God as everything. But the words, 'Dare to look further' acted as a focal point, which coalesced the expansive feelings of bliss and love into a transparent calm. A calmness that was the clear seeing that,

"Everything comes from nothing."

'Nothing' in the sense that it is 'not-a-thing,' not an object. This nothingness is the ultimate subject from which everything manifests.

I was dumbfounded with this clear seeing, it was a knowing without thinking that contained no doubt or uncertainty, simply a self-evident truth. No thoughts arose, there was just the resting in—and as—this truth. I cannot say for how long this lasted, as it was outside of time. Nothing can be said of this nothingness, as there is no-thing there to describe. Yet everything was present. This nothingness was beyond mind and all description, just a deep, knowing awareness without anything known.

My gaze then fell to Mother Amma and the knowing modulated into a love without limits. I felt there was nothing or no one that I could not love. This love was a continual forgiveness in the light that all was God. The vibration of this love had no boundary in a sea of unity, on and on I sank in this love of all. My heart seemed to expand in the warmth of all as divine.

There then came a light that beckoned from the photo of Ramana, as his eyes seemed to glisten. The strangest of all sinking feelings came over me silently, without any effort or resistance; it was the realisation that there was just 'No me.'

This was the mercy blow, the *coup de grâce*. There was nothing to hold on to and no centre to hold from, just a limitless awareness beyond description.

There was no one to deny, nor nothing to deny, yet all was and that 'all' was nothing.

I was unborn.

I later saw that I had been sitting at the altar for seven hours. Gradually some thoughts had surfaced. One of the first was,

"I am awakened."

With this thought came a huge belly laugh of mirth at the vagaries of language and the folly of attempted reclamation. For indeed it had just been seen that there was 'no me,' the separate personal 'I' simply did not exist, so how could 'I' be awakened? Awakening is not personal, as it is totally un-possessed. Awake-ness is ever-present awareness of what is. A separate person can never awaken. Awareness simply stops identifying with the limited form of body-mind as a separate entity.

Another thought that arose as a fear was that 'I' might lose this, like before, but I smiled in recognition that there was no one to lose this realisation nor was there anyone to hold on to this realisation. Waves of gratitude flooded my body, even to say 'my' body is not fully true as there was no 'me' to make it 'mine' but for the sake of description we require language, so I use the words without a sense of ownership.

The here and now shone as a bright, clear awareness, as a deep, knowing being. I could see that at the first awakening, I had been swept away in the bliss of unity but that the 'me' had rolled along in a wave of appropriation that had re-veiled that very same unity. This time however, the realisation of 'no-self' had revealed that identification with the inside centre of 'me' was but a play of thoughts, emotions, beliefs and opinions held together in a smoke screen of past tendencies and conditioning; a momentum of becoming, arising and falling movements that gave the appearance of being a separate and solid individual. It was an illusory 'me' that needed constant identification and attention to fuel its façade.

Losing identity

Now it might seem that this would be the end of the story, that this realisation would wipe the slate clean immediately, in a sweep of nothingness that would make everything whole and perfect. One might believe that nothing could assuage the ivory tower of this absolute truth and indeed this may be the case for some, that all their latent tendencies, conditioning and patterns get swept away permanently in one realisation.

Yet it would appear that there are many different ways that awakening unfolds. So much energy had gone into spinning the story of 'me' that even with the centre seen through, there were still elements of the story spinning around the periphery. These remaining elements of emotions and thoughts still had a charge and a momentum that came to the surface with a sticky magnetism, which at times could be overwhelming and could bring about temporary re-identification. Yet these too were just a movement in the overall awakening and it was in the daily affairs of bills, work, relationships and obligations that the remaining patterns of the separate individual 'me' were flushed to the surface.

The truth of 'no-self' is a living truth, an embodiment in the everyday world, with all its ups and downs—an embodiment that is not a practice but a spontaneous, grounded unfolding. I began to see that it was really just the beginning, the start of a new phase. The dance of 'me and you' had come to a halt, but a new tune had emerged as a singular waltz of 'no-self' and 'no-other'—an embodied flow of life that dances through all and meets any resistance with open arms.

Awakening itself is not a process—it is a spontaneous, intuitive knowing that is not bound by time or space, yet there can be a movement after an awakening where remaining resistances are brought to the surface to be seen.

There are no defined, sequential, progressive steps after such a clear seeing. Yet there is an unfolding that depends on the environment, conditions and resistances that are met. Our own inner truth is the compass by which each unfolding is best undertaken.

One of the first things I noticed after this clear seeing, was that I would only sleep a couple of hours a night. It was as if the energetic tension that had been held as a contraction in the body was now freed up, resulting in the body feeling energised with a palpable aliveness. This had the effect that I did not need as much sleep to recharge and so the lack of sleep was no real problem. This equalised within a few months and there returned a similar duration of sleep, albeit with a different quality.

For days after this seeing, there was a simple joy in being and a real clarity to perception. Life was revealed as a transparent bliss without cause. In fact, no reason was needed, as there was no questioner of this transparency. All was just incredibly all right. There was a calmness and peace that was beyond logic.

Nonetheless, over time, I was aware of 'me' thoughts linked to subtle tensions re-emerging in the body-mind. There was an urge to deny these thoughts and feelings, to ignore them with the truth that there was 'no-self' here that could be bothered. Yet the truth spoke of absolute transparency and here were tensions related to thoughts in the field of attention. Real or not, these emotions and thoughts were calling out—to deny them would be just another form of resistance and control.

It can be quite a jar to witness the re-emergence of old, held beliefs and feelings, knots of resistance to unity, knots that had, for so long, given one the impression of a separate self. The very personal nature of these patterns can have a gravitational pull that threatens to re-identify one with a limited, little 'me.'

Here the temptation is to, 'Stay away! Keep away!' as if these patterns are a dangerous plague that may sully or vanquish the truth of 'no-self.'

These patterns can seem repugnant in their stickiness, yet the truth of awakening is an unconditional love that is fearless in its openness. If we try to fixate on any position, including any truth, as a means to avoid, then we are attempting to restrict the flow of truth. But the light of truth always shines on all, without prejudice or favour. A fixation on the truth of 'no-self' can turn into a dry concept, used to hide from what is deemed undesirable when perception is still driven by personal craving and aversion.

Even the term 'truth of no-self' is not ultimately true, for the Truth can never be put into words. To know this and to recognise that the egoic-mind's nature is to fixate and conceptualise is of great value. For to know how the egoic-mind weaves itself is a key to bringing consciousness to unconscious holding patterns. The seeing of how the illusory 'me' builds itself is the very dispelling of its ability to pull one into delusion and limited identification. The magic trick of 'me' loses its alluring power when we see its machinations—thus undoing the spell of trance in transparency.

I later came to learn that these latent tendencies or patterns were called *vasanas* or *samskaras*—imprints or patterns that seemed to keep one in illusion, tied to the karmic wheel of samsara. I had read some Buddhist literature many years before and I had intellectually understood from it that craving and aversion were the root cause of suffering.

Yet what became clear to me is that craving and aversion, or desiring and fearing, are movements around an imagined separate centre of 'me' or 'I'—a belief in an autonomous entity. It is this fictional 'me,' which seems to issue decrees of what is desirable or feared. What is desirable is seen to enhance the 'me,' and what is feared is seen as a threat to the 'me.'

It is a constant pushing away or pulling towards that gives propulsion and validity to this separate 'me,' a 'me' that is always trying to become finally happy by gaining what it wants and avoiding what it does not want. This illusory 'me,' or 'I' thought, could be seen to be the central reference point, with fear and desire being the centrifugal forces—constantly spinning and creating the appearance of substantiality. The illusion of a seemingly separate, inner subject of 'me,' which is always desiring or avoiding outer objects as a means to happiness and peace in a continual effort to bring about satisfaction.

Here identification with subject-object dualism spins a web of illusion that maintains itself by belief in a separate self. Karma appears to be a collection of imprints, desires and fears, held as a moving pattern that continually spins in an attempt to find fulfilment.

Yet the storehouse of karma is being constantly added to, like a stage play in which each actor continually extends the play by assuming the position of playwright—a self-generating script that keeps the roles perpetually in motion.

I came to see that karmic patterns unfold for the body-mind, yet we are not limited to the body-mind. Our true nature is that which gives rise to all of manifestation. What we are is beyond all personal karma as the witnessing of all temporal expressions and experiences.

This was a vital point in the unfolding, for it would be easy to use awakening as an escape—to dive into the emptiness of 'no-self' as a means to avoid limitation and contraction in an attempt to gain and hold *nirvana* by shunning samsara. But this would simply be trading one side of duality for the other. I was beginning to see the emptiness and totality of non-duality, in that samsara is the appearance of nirvana when we are no longer identified with division or separation in any way. Samsara and nirvana are not two separate realms. As paradoxical as it may seem, samsara is nirvana and nirvana is samsara. To try rid oneself of samsara is the very movement of craving and aversion that keeps one tied to the wheel of illusory suffering with the belief that samsara is somehow separate and not part of divine unity. It is only when one no longer argues or identifies with samsara in an attempt to control the flow of life that there is a true surrender—a total relinquishing of the belief in separation that then reveals the Reality of non-duality. This is intimately conveyed in the Buddhist Heart Sutra,

"Form is emptiness; emptiness is form."

It became evident that the constriction I had been feeling before this awakening was the rattling of my conceptual framework. The separate 'me' that I had thought to be so real had been in the spotlight, a self-interrogation with the inquiry, 'Who or what am I?'

The sustained desire for truth was the light that had crumbled this imagined, separate centre. Yet the centrifugal forces of craving and aversion were still spinning, attempting to define an empty centre and reweave a 'subjective me.' But without the identifying attention of belief that fuels such motion, it is just a matter of time before the curtain falls.

It is much like a small whirlwind or dust devil in which the wind patterns have moved centripetally so as to pull in and push away debris, lending it a temporary solidity as it moves along. Yet at no time is it ever separate from the environment as a totality.

In reality, it is not a matter of getting rid of these patterns or past tendencies, but of allowing them to be, without trying to control or manipulate them. Even saying allowing them could be misunderstood, as indeed there is no separate person to allow. It is a matter of no agenda and no control; it is just an openness to what is. These patterns, which are consciousness too, have been in contraction for so long, it is as if they need to come up for air, to breathe unhindered by suppression.

This is where the body or kinaesthetic sense of self can be a great ally, as past tendencies can be felt as a tension or discord in the body and inner-body awareness alerts us to the presence of any disharmony or discord. This discord can be felt from the grossest to the subtlest way in any part of the body, but can often be most noticeable in the areas of the head, the heart and the solar plexus. These are not separate, demarcated zones but rather overlapping areas of engagement. They correspond to the intellectual, emotional and physical, respectively.

We have all had experiences of disharmony in these areas—our head can be a fog of confusion, our heart can close down in grief, or our gut can become a knot of rage at times. All patterns of resistance show themselves in the body when there is a lack of harmony with what is. They can be felt as an emotion, sensation, or tension in the body and generally have a belief structure or memory associated with them. Each pattern has a story, so to speak; a fear, desire, memory, or belief that defines the 'me,' past, present and future. These disharmonies are a signal to bring our attention to the fact that there is discord and can be a means to harmony when we welcome them, in openness.

It is in the simple welcoming openness, akin to a deep listening, where any disharmony may be heard. In the hearing of it there is no denial or identification with it, no craving or aversion, just a willingness to allow all to be as it is. Any disharmony may then unfold without containment and perhaps even dissipate, although this is not the aim.

The goal is not to rid oneself of the unpleasant. The welcoming openness is a love of truth that witnesses all without judgment, giving any disharmony time and space without agenda. Associated thoughts, emotions and memories may arise with bodily sensations; these too are just allowed to be. For awareness itself is an openness that is already allowing all to be and has always been allowing all to be. Its nature is uncontrolled acceptance. I found myself simply resting back more and more, into and as this openness, as it was seen that all that arises is already free to be or not to be. This allowing is a clear seeing without attraction or revulsion.

What is happening is that awareness is being brought to an unconscious holding pattern. Here the simple welcoming, or equanimity, does not lend attention to the movements of craving and aversion with the result that there is no fuelling of the egoic structure.

In the silent, open awareness itself there is an intuitive intelligence, an intelligence that can see to the heart of any holding with spontaneous clarity. The light of truth dispels all holding in its own transparency.

No guilt without pride

Life at this time was a constant invitation to surrender, as past beliefs and long-held emotions floated to the surface from the diffuse depths of the infallible-unexamined. Throughout this time there was an ebb and flow, a harmonising movement of absolute and relative values. Often there would be temporary re-identifications with old patterns, which felt like putting on an ill-fitting suit from childhood. While, at other times, the clear and transparent truth of 'no-self' would shine through, saturating my being with a peace that could hold no argument with that moment. This revisiting was revitalising, like the breath of air as you reach the surface after a long dive on a fresh, warm day.

This transformation was woven into the daily chores of work and play and took its own rhythm. I was blessed with the freedom to be alone, as I worked making drums and rattles or completing the tasks of life on a small farm. Often for weeks I would not see another person except for my wife.

The man-made world of politics, wars, dramas and television were not within my field of vision, yet more and more I saw the root of their numbing allure. A huge game of opinions based on assumed rights and wrongs that becomes a battlefield, both personally and collectively: 'our' versus 'your.'

The only difference between 'our' and 'your,' but a simple 'y.'

A 'y' that begs the question,

"Why?"

All these 'ours' are but a collection of 'me's seeking continuation in the play of other; the belief in a 'me' extending out to what is 'mine.'

Boundaries of extending identity that seem to separate 'me' from 'you,' but what is 'yours,' I may also desire or fear—the craving and aversion of an egoic structure projecting a world of division and imagined boundaries—billons of little 'me's agreeing and disagreeing on conceptual boundaries.

Separate and collective worlds of thought colliding in desire and fear, creating conflict around the personal and collective illusory dichotomy of gain and loss, spinning around the empty centre of 'me.' A contagious belief of 'me-ness' causing physical, psychological and emotional suffering, turning a magical display of diversity into a nightmare of suffering separation.

Yet this is how consciousness is manifesting and I can now see no wrong or right in it. I am reminded of a saying which advises to be wary of denying any person their suffering, least you deny them their awakening. And I can attest to this, in that in my own life it was often at the hardest moments that I came to question the very nature of reality and in these moments I felt the strongest orientation towards home. This may not only be true on the individual level, it may be relevant on the collective level also. Yet surrender does not have to come about through suffering alone, there are those who offer little resistance to life and slip back into their true nature with ease, like a small wave in the deep ocean that is gently pulled back into the depths without a ripple.

We all, from time to time, get spontaneous moments of 'no-self' where the little 'me' is taking a break. Selfless being and action arise from this non-separation, without any thoughts of end-gaining, in a flow of life that is not held as it washes over all imagined boundaries. This is where true love, compassion, gratitude, humility and happiness shine through, giving a taste of our natural state of openness—a glimpse of no-boundary where the thought of 'me' has given way to open, clear awareness that is intensely alive as a deep, intuitive knowing beyond words and thoughts. These tastes of 'no-self' are pointers to the possibilities of life without identification with contraction or separation. These glimpses can come in a multitude of ways, but all sing of unity.

    I learned a deep lesson on the illusory nature of division one day as I worked on the farm. We kept chickens and ducks and, towards the end of autumn, we found homes for many of the ducklings that had hatched in spring. Invariably, the excess males were not homed, so we decided to harvest them for food. It was a job I had done before and could find no wrong in, as in nature there is constant predation—the cycle of birth and death that is inseparable from life. Before I had to do this job again, I re-examined the situation from the perspective of 'no-self,' that all was consciousness and that there was nothing separate. If everything was divine consciousness, then whether it is a duck or a carrot, it is all made from the same consciousness. They were equally divine and no distinction could be made. Still, there was something I could not quite put my finger on—a slight unease in my body. Yet on I went and as I worked on those four birds there came a thought that gripped me:

"At what point does life leave the body?"

As I worked I could see blood leave those bodies as their movements came to an end, yet I could not pinpoint when life left the body. Even as I held the carcasses, I could not tell if life had left or not.

As I divided up each body into feathers, feet, head, flesh and entrails, the question deepened and took on an intensity that took hold in my body.

"What was I dividing up?"

I could not tell where life ended, nor could I tell if life could be divided. I had seen that life is one consciousness and that there is nothing that is truly separate. Yet the questioning had arose and I wondered at what point did consciousness leave the body. My mind simply could not get a grip on this, I could not actually say at what point this happened, even as I watched each bird stop moving and their eyes glaze over. The questioning gripped me with a ferocity that I could not turn from. Gradually I started to see that it was pointing to an unexamined belief I held that consciousness resides in the body. I began to see the consensus belief that I had assumed and that this was a belief that the vast majority of people hold. It was that consciousness is a product of our brain functions. It held that consciousness is in the brain, the brain is in the body and the body is in the world.

Yet I had seen that all is consciousness, hence it cannot be contained nor can it leave, as it is ever-present and infinite. Where would or could it go? There can be nothing outside of the infinite!

What could contain the infinite?

A brain?

A body?

This questioning stayed with me for days. There had been a clear seeing of 'no-self' but this was still filtering down and meeting all resistances on the mental, emotional and physical levels. I could see that there was still, very much, a bodily sense of a 'me' in here and a world out there. My body got tenser and tenser over the days with a defending unease.

As I lay in bed one morning, I wondered had I done wrong by killing the birds. No sooner than this thought arose, there came a deep pulse, like a wave of knowing energy that shook my body, the knowing came as a clear voice that said,

"I have never done anything wrong!"

With that my mind went blank as my body vibrated with this seeing. The truth of 'no-self' began to flush up memories that were held like coiled patterns within the body. Memories of all the things I had believed that I had done wrong in life started to unfold. Each memory had a specific emotional charge that could be felt as a tension or feeling in the body which could elicit another thought or memory. These thoughts attempted to contain, condemn, or grade wrongness with shame and secrecy—yet these too were witnessed without identification or ownership. It was a flood of letting go that was beyond control.

After some time I got up for breakfast, feeling as light as a feather, without a care in the world. I was smiling like an innocent child, unburdened by self-recrimination. As I sat drinking my coffee, the other shoe dropped. A gentle voice arose inside,

"I have never done anything right!"

This was actually shocking. It was great to be free of all the messy stuff, but the shiny stuff was definitely mine, or so I believed. To let go of all that I liked about myself, all the perceived accomplishments, praises, victories and successes, all of the right choices and judgments which formed what was best about me: the shiny self-image. Yet as I sat, they slowly unwound in the light of truth and ever-present awareness. These memories, thoughts and feelings of 'me' that were held were but temporary waves in a limitless sea of awareness, waves that were never truly separate. To hold on to them was a limiting of consciousness to a perception, to fixate a 'me' in time and space, an illusory divorce from all that is.

I simply sat, witnessing personal right and wrong dissolve in the transparency of 'no-self'—the untarnished stillness of truth. I began to see more deeply into the advice that Mother Meera had given in her book, which was to offer everything up to the divine, good or bad, as the divine finds nothing distasteful.

I could see the truth that the limitless, aware presence was beyond right and wrong. To surrender one's deeds, thoughts, feelings and memories was self-surrender. A letting go of a fixation—the relative perspective of 'me'—this was a dissolving of duality.

Here was a true absolution, forgiveness in the dissolution of the conditioned patterns of 'me,' as consciousness shines on unconsciousness without any notion of right or wrong, just a unifying embrace of 'no me' and 'no you' in a dispersal of illusion.

The infinite mystery chooses

This dissolution of apparent polar opposites played out over weeks. Resistances were felt like players running out on stage for one last hurrah when the audience has already left the building. This realisation, that I had never done anything right or wrong, really brought a deeper questioning of doer-ship. If I had indeed never done anything right or wrong, then had I, in fact, ever done anything? Had I ever even been the doer?

The belief in being 'the doer' is really the same as the belief in being the 'separate-personal-self,' yet it had been seen that there was 'no-self.' I really struggled with this at times, as it pointed to the possibility that I had never done anything, that all my personal history was but a story referenced from an imaginary position called 'me.'

'I,' as a personal doer, would seem to be a fiction. This, in turn, raised questions about the nature of free will, effort and choice that were truly staggering.

As I sat with my wife one day, drinking tea and chatting, there came a flow of knowing inner words,

"I have no mother, I have no father,

I have no wife, I have no brother,

I have no sisters, I have no children."

These words arose internally without volition, like a mantra of undoing from the vast unknown silence, it continued,

"I am not a son, I am not a husband,

I am not a brother and I am not a father."

The truth of the unborn was meeting all of my identified roles with a force that was unstoppable and undoubtable from the perspective of 'no-self.' Far from being a diminishment, there arose a deep love and gratitude, as if the very fabric of life itself was a love without argument or loss. I just continued to drink my tea and smiled over to my wife in recognition of the beauty of that moment and the love of life exactly as it was. It is curious as one surrenders to the truth of 'no-self,' there comes an expansion that can allow for paradox, subtly and gently, without conflict, as two seemingly different perspectives can be occupied.

This realisation of not being the separate doer brought on an intensification of presence and a deepening surrender. As I worked around the farm the 'I' would become lost in the totality of being, where even the space between objects was scintillating with life: one life. The distance between objects was no longer empty but full with a pregnancy of being that was a unifying force of 'no other.' The trees, shovel, plants, dogs, wind and rain all sang as consciousness, a simplicity of being that expressed an intelligence beyond measure in a dazzling display of diversity. At such moments, thoughts would drop away and there would just be feeling, seeing, hearing, smelling, without reference to an 'I'—a timelessness of being without a centre of reference, without the personal experiencer. The whole environment would take on a beautiful, dream-like quality as a lucidity permeated all without exception.

These moments themselves seemed to come and go in their own harmonising way, beyond any personal control. At times, when the oneness was veiled, one could slip into the feeling that it had been lost, yet nothing was amiss and nothing needed to be chased. Consciousness was in the driving seat with destination unknown. At times the body-mind identity would vie for control, but with the car, map, fuel, road and world all being consciousness, what could be done? In this openness the mind would not be engaged, though afterwards there could be a movement of mind that would elicit a need to categorise and label in an effort to make known the unknowable—but to no avail. Bit by bit the mind began to recognise its own inability to appropriate what was beyond it. The mind-dominated, relative world of objects in time and space could not come to bear on the here and now of the infinite, only bow in acquiescence to the unknown and unknowable. Here is where the personal doer would be subsumed into the flow of being, the spontaneous happening of totality without cause.

Free will was but the illusion of choice based on a separate 'me.' While consciousness is the player of all forms, it is also consciousness that is the chooser. It can choose to become identified with a body-mind object and in so doing it ignores its limitlessness to take on a limited form. This ignoring is the basis of the illusion of ignorance, which can be said to be the identification of consciousness with a limited form. Perhaps even the word 'chooser' is too strong a word; instead, one might say that it is the flowering of consciousness in human form that brings about temporary identification. It is also consciousness that chooses to dis-identify from form and awaken to it itself. This is why awakening is never personal. It is, in fact, the negation of the person as a separate individual. The words attributed to Jesus sum up self-surrender so beautifully,

"Thy will, not mine, be done,"

These words speak of letting go of the belief in personal control, personal free will, personal choice and personal doer-ship—where thy will is my will.

Even the seeming choice or effort to surrender is but the truth and light of divinity blossoming in form. As awareness becomes aware of itself, consciousness as contracted form stops denying its limitlessness. The feeling and belief that consciousness is in the brain, which is in the body, which is in the world began to re-orientate as consciousness was experienced to be infinite and ever-present. It was actually the opposite of what had been believed; the brain, body and world are in consciousness and this unbroken consciousness is our natural, open state.

The answer to the question raised when harvesting the ducks had become self-evident. Consciousness never leaves the body, as it is the body that is within consciousness. Birth and death are inseparable aspects to manifestation, but what gives breath to it all is consciousness and consciousness has no beginning and no end—it is unborn and undying—and we are that one, undivided consciousness.

I could see how the truth of 'no-self' was moving to meet all mental, emotional and physical resistances. Beliefs, feelings and sensations that claimed, 'I am the body-mind,' were being met with a transparency that left no ground on which the separate, personal individual could stand. I was in free fall. More and more I began to feel this truth permeate mind and body. I would experience waves of energy flood throughout the body, sometimes pleasurable, sometimes not, with a vibrational intensity that was, at times, so strong I would have to grab hold of a wall or chair to stabilise myself until it passed.

In the seeing of no-self there can be a transcendence as we no longer identify with the separate body-mind apparatus, for we see that our essential nature is unconditioned. After this dis-identification from limited form, we may then come to appreciate that we are the appearance of all phenomena, including the body-mind, as an undivided expression of the totality

Around this time, I lost the desire to harvest and eat meat, not because I could see anything wrong in it, but quite simply it just fell away. I found, as my body sensitised, I could no longer eat meat; the energetic vibration of it would pull me off balance for days. My diet had naturally adjusted itself as the body had harmonised to what was needed during this period.

My altar is emptied

At this time I got the chance to travel to London to have darshan with Mother Meera. The journey to London was somewhat of a jolt to the system, as I had been tucked away for months in the wild and natural seclusion of our farm. It was like entering another world as I travelled into the unending bombardment of people, advertising, noise and activity. The sheer frenetic pace held such a pull on my attention, as if it had the power to lure 'me' out into the busyness of becoming. It was a bit like an ex-alcoholic walking into the wildest free bar and watching the mayhem. I felt traces of old patterns come to the surface, noting that when desire and aversion get attached to perceiving, they act as a fuel to bolster the illusory, psychological self. Without a belief in a central, separate 'me,' these old patterns of becoming arose and fell in the witnessing presence, only momentarily pulling. Without a tether to the 'me' they could not re-identify attention to the objects of desire and aversion.

So many of the faces I saw gave the impression of containment, as if all of these people were locked in their own private little worlds of limited identity. Yet at the same time, there was a great beauty to it all; the unlimited emptiness manifesting in a display of smiles, music, buildings, growls and smog.

After having moved through this hectic play of life, to then sit at the feet of the Divine Mother was a salve of stillness. So often before, when visiting Mother Meera, I would inwardly ask for help with a specific issue. Gradually though, I came to realise that all was already in hand. To simply sit in her presence generated a resonance in which holding and resistance were exposed and dissolved in the clear light of Paramatman; a clear, unobstructed embodiment of the divine is a unique and powerful gift to all of manifestation.

It was strange, yet totally natural, that during this period of harmonisation I had, more and more, let go of the altar at which I had worked for many years. It had been a place of refuge from the vicissitudes of life and a focal point of the divine for me for so long. It was a place of undoing and devotion, where I looked to the teachers there present as my guides—mirrors wherein I could see where I was held. However, this awakening of 'no-self' had de-stabilised the belief that 'I' was separate from the divine. In so doing, everything was revealed to be the altar of the divine—there was no moving to or from the divine, as all was divine. The entire world was a sacrament, a manifestation of divine glory that I was in no way separate from. I was beginning to let go of the idea that only some specific forms, places, or people were sacred.

Yet there had still been an inner pull that had brought me to London to sit with the form of Mother Meera and in her presence I understood why. As I sat in silence a huge doubt arose in me like a torrent of accusation,

"Is all this for real, are you for real?"

As this came to the surface I immediately felt an urge to deny this thought and feeling, to quench it quickly with my years of devotion. How could I have such notions? Yet I knew the wisdom in not suppressing, there is strength in withholding nothing and offering everything up to the divine—the Mother lovingly accepts all gifts from her children. Awareness is the substratum of all and it resists nothing, as nothing is unpalatable or impermissible. The holding of doubt aloft was the opening of the heart to all, without favour. This remaining doubt was offered up, it was the movement of seeing the world as illusory, because when the 'me' collapses, the belief in a separate world of objects also begins to crumble and all is seen as divine, all is seen as God or unity consciousness. It is beautifully put by the Indian sage Shankara:

"The world is illusion,

Brahman alone is real,

Brahman is the world."

This doubt spoke of seeing the world of separation as illusion and of coming to understand that God was the one Reality. This was just part of the movement of harmonising truth, there was also the celebration of 'God as the unified appearance of multiplicity' to follow.

I had travelled to London and back but, in reality, if all was consciousness and the body-mind was within consciousness, had I even taken one step? It was just like an actor in a film who appears to be moving, yet never moves from the display of the TV screen. Similarly, on the screen of consciousness the character of 'me' had appeared to travel to London to sit with Mother Meera. All there was, in reality, was consciousness—consciousness as 'me,' consciousness as London and consciousness as Mother Meera. Yet this was the appearance of movement and harmonisation that consciousness had chosen to take. The dis-play of 'me' and Mother was deepening beyond form as an unresisting stillness; consciousness as the substratum of all came to the foreground and the paradox of embracing no other was felt in gratitude. More and more, 'I' came to rest back as this consciousness, as identification with the body-mind lessened.

For weeks after this visit there came an ease and a flow that could be described as a warming of the heart. Waves of love and gratitude would wash over me. It was not a love and a gratitude for anything in particular but was felt as a modulation of the ever-present life force—a taste of natural, open presence. Old patterns of appropriation would arise and try to claim these feeling as personal, but it was akin to trying to grasp water while being submerged in it, all the while the submersion of self was the melting of the frozen image of an icy 'me.'

A couple of weeks after this, I got a chance to attend my first *satsang*. It was with Stuart Schwartz. Satsang is a term that can be said to mean 'association with truth' and is where people gather with the shared intent of truth and presence. As we drove there, I became aware of a pain in my heart that felt more energetic than physical that increased the closer we got to our destination. It was refreshing that the satsang was held in a sitting room, without fanfare or regalia, without any hint of a pedestal or any show of outer mysticism. There was just an air of friendliness, of people getting together to explore their own inherent nature. It was interesting to note the depth of presence that transpired as the meeting went on. It was as if the combined love of truth stripped away pretence and illusion, turning attention inwards, revealing the depth of awareness in the moment. Stuart guided people to unmask their emotional and psychological patterns of holding and resistance with sincerity, humour and grace.

As I took my place, the pain in my heart swelled until, at times, it seemed to contain the whole world. I could see it as a pattern of intricate, moving light and the intensity of it felt like it would break through my chest at any moment. As I talked to Stuart, the pain coalesced to a pinpoint, like a fine thread knot at the heart, though at the same time seeming to be without locale. In this meeting there was a witnessing of this heart-knot, which seemed to wink in and out of existence, as if it were both existent and non-existent. The associated pain around this began to dissipate in the openness without agenda. It was a valuable lesson in the art of undoing.

I later came across a term, *hridaya granthi*, used by Indian sages, which is said to be the point at the heart that is the source of the 'I' thought—a knot of self-contraction that, when undone, leads to the realisation of non-dual awareness. I began to see the similarities between this reference and what I had been experiencing.

The Non Jewel

Eluding to this pearl is
But a poetic dance
Which may unveil the light
Of no mind in no one
But only at the very moment
That words undo
As if void of volition
A silent truth
That never dies
I alone am
A boundless sea
Of unconditioned love
Unborn
Ever anew

Un-possessed radiance

Before this seeing of 'no-self,' which had been driven by the questioning of identity and protection, I found that my work with the mapacho had just fallen away. The work with it had brought me to question my very existence as a limited, separate individual. This awakening however, had shown that there was no separate self to protect. The clear truth of this began to filter down in a process of dissolution of the emotional, intellectual and physical holding that was still at play. There came an open, clarifying awareness to meet the old, protective patterns of 'me' and 'mine.' These moving patterns were like defence mechanisms made of beliefs, thoughts, feelings and opinions—a circular armour around the core belief of me—much like the medieval suits of armour hanging in museums as empty shells protecting nought but emptiness. When these old patterns arose they could be witnessed on an energetic level as surges in the body that would evoke emotional and mental responses. At times there would be the pull of re-identification as the conceptual 'me' attempted to cloud the truth of 'no-self.'

Yet without constant identification, which is a fuelling, these patterns began to dissolve. Old triggering agents of people and events were a disarming gift. Like remote bomb detectors they would detonate the hidden mines, or mine's within the playground of 'me'—a bombastic zone of reactivity. After awakening, I found I was not fully and permanently immune to such temporary re-identifications. There remained certain, held misperceptions as fixation points that needed to be seen. I knew the arising of these conditionings to be the unwinding of the separate body-mind system. Yet often, as the old patterns and re-identifications happened, they were, in fact, felt even more deeply, as if a fall from grace had occurred and one had slipped back into the mire. Yet it was actually grace itself at work in this dissolution— grace as the truth of the timeless moment of instantaneous awakening descending in a process of harmonisation, moving one beyond the gravitational force of the separate-self state.

The fallout of this radical dissolution often felt like fear and grief, as one felt a dying to all that was once held so dear. It was nakedness in the face of a hurricane without hold or hiding place. This fierce grace pointed out all the old patterns of contraction, flushing them out in the daily grind and polish of life. I began to see that there was no outside agent capable of veiling my true nature. The only veiling agent was the seemingly separate 'me.' The remaining threads of my separate, individual life were like a frayed prayer flag, fading to nothing in the totality of an impersonal life. I saw that there is nothing to be gained in awakening for the separate individual, except the demise of all imaginary-personal, egoic structures. It was the ending of 'my' world.

More and more, I began to pinpoint the particular thoughts, beliefs and feelings wherein I un-awakened myself to the trance of separation. These fixation points were like buttons of self-activation, which tied one to the karmic body-mind that is bound by the law of cause and effect—a dream of inner division. It can be hard to witness one's behaviour in a display that we know not to be true—as if driven by inner, unseen forces. To know the truth of 'no-self' and yet to act in an untrue manner can sometimes be disheartening, but these temporary re-identifications are just spontaneous happenings and can be seen to be a universal occurrence that we may or may not identify with. It is the love of truth that loosens the moorings of identification. A sincerity that does not let one hide out in the memory of an awakening but brings the truth to meet any resistance in the moment. It is the integrity to know the real, at all costs, regardless of the outcome. Here then the ebb and flow of identification and re-identification can be seen to be the dissolving of the residues of ignorance.

Radical honesty prevents the fixation of the ego to the truth of 'no-self' as a means to deny whatever is arising. It does not maintain the stance of a solely conceptual understanding of 'no-self' as a way to deny un-awakened behaviour with the excuse,

"It was not me because there is not me."

Honesty moves to meet all those contractions and beliefs with which we un-awaken ourselves. All limitations are met and embraced as no other and dissolve in the love of truth. The very nature of awakening is compassion, which does not avoid or seek to change; it simply and fearlessly allows all to be as it is. The clarity of this transparency offers no resistance and without resistance, these old patterns cannot maintain their cohesion. In unattached witnessing we do not come to claim or deny, as unconditional love shows everything to be already whole.

It may seem challenging to stay as this uncontrolled openness when, for so long, attention has gone to maintaining the bastion of 'me.' Yet at times it is possible that we do not close down in anger, shame, fear, greed, rage, or guilt. We then begin to witness all thoughts, emotions and perceptions as part of an impersonal totality. This vantage allows all these emotions, thoughts and sensations to arise and fall without ownership. They wash through, as a wave, without holding. All 'arisings' are seen to be like waves on the surface of an endless ocean, where we are both the ocean and the waves. The process of dis-identification is the de-limiting of attention from a wave back to its wholeness as the ocean. The characteristics of the wave may remain or change, but from the infinite stillness of the deep ocean, it is not separate and not so turbulent.

As this non-resistance deepens, one becomes more aware of the depth and stillness, becoming less and less swayed by temporary squalls. I cannot say I was always untouched by the weathering of daily life, yet such re-identifications were precious pointers to the anchor-points of the separate 'me.' What is important after such moments of re-identification is not to go into a secondary spiral of self-confirming recrimination. To reproach oneself is to maintain identification with this limited, separate self. I came to see that it is just as important to accept these moments as equally valid, to see truly that all of these movements are beyond personal control.

Forgiveness could be said to be the relinquishment of all judgments of self and other, an openness to whatever is, forgiveness in which we do not identify with any limited position. It does not imply a lack of discernment or action, which is a natural function of life. Discernment gives rise to appropriate and spontaneous action in any situation, but forgiveness is that by which all is allowed to be, an unconditional love for each moment where there is, in reality, nothing to forgive. I was beginning to see the unifying truth and power of this love and I learned a valuable lesson in the unconditioned from the light and love of Mother Amma, whom I went to see at this time.

As I attended the event, there arose the sting of old patterns of judging. The intensity of the living, moving presence of thousands of people in a dance of seeking, prayer, unity, frustration, celebration and devotion had a resonance that flushed old patterns to the surface. All of these people had come to be embraced by the embodied, unconditional love of the Mother. I noticed throughout the day that there arose a limiting labelling of people and also the remembrance of old labelling from previous commentaries as I encountered familiar faces.

To divide and categorise is the nature of the mind, a labelling and defining of multiplicity. Along with this can come an ingrained, egoic colouring of craving and aversion in a measured glance of superior and inferior. So much of my own conditioning was the judgments and images I held of others, labels like 'interesting,' 'useful,' 'fun,' 'nasty,' 'boring…' Labels I had assigned to people and events in my life, which in fact said more about me than they did about the other.

These were really the illusory bars of 'my' separateness. The 'me' stands as judge and every judgment bolsters and reinforces its own position as the one who knows or wants to know. The dualistic split of subject-object, 'me and you' divides itself out into a myriad of images and categorisations. This judging can even turn in on itself in the form of self-judgments and criticisms. All pronouncements, judgments and opinions are but an attempted splintering of life based on the existence of a separate 'me,'—a 'me' that creates the seeming other. And all judgements, regardless of their flavour, are simply to enhance the self-image, the shimmering 'me' that we believe ourselves to be.

As I sat and watched these patterns, a prayer arose to the Divine Mother, a divine which was not separate but which was more clearly expressed and seen in the radiance and grace of Mother Amma. I asked for the help to see past these limiting judgements. Then, as my turn came to receive her embrace, there came a downloading of a vibrating, energetic stream that grew in intensity as I approached her form. It was like I was being rebooted and this became crystallised in her arms. As I came away and sat in wordless silence, the room took on a luminescence that highlighted the inherent radiance of all the people and faces I could see. Everyone was seen to be intensely beautiful and all eyes shone with a light. I recognised that what was looking through all of those eyes was the exact same presence that was looking through my eyes, one awareness looking through all eyes and every eye was the eye of the divine. God shone through all eyes alike, without favour or exception.

I was coming to see the limitless, ever-present beauty in all. What limiting judgement could hold true in the infinite eye of God? The intensity of this gradually diminished within minutes, yet the perfume of it still remains as a feeling of the limitless love that is our true nature.

Although an awakening may show that there is no personal, psychological self or no separation, there is still the living of this knowledge and the harmonisation of it in all aspects: emotionally, physically and intellectually. In the presence of a Self-Realised being, a resonance comes into play, a transmission that can re-orchestrate our held identity and give us a deepening glimpse beyond the veil of separation in a harmony that is breathtaking in beauty and majesty.

Flowering home

A similar dropping-away happened when working with the plants as a means of seeking wholeness. I had been listening to a talk by Adyashanti one evening as I washed the dishes. He was elucidating the words of Meister Eckhart on how the one who sees casts no shadow. As soon as I heard these words it felt as if the back of my head blew open energetically. The sense of solidity behind the eyes vanished; there was no one behind or separate. An expansiveness opened up that continued to broaden. More and more, I would find myself sitting, not in meditation, but simply sitting without choice, a settling from the activity of mind and body without control or purpose as a natural expression of that moment.

It was a resting as open awareness rather than a striving to get to a perfect silence. As I sat in such a manner one evening after this, I strongly felt the presence of Mother Amma and Mother Meera, while at the same time the very visceral sense of inhabiting the head shifted and settled at the heart centre. It was a move from intellectual understanding to heart wisdom and with it came a wordless warmth. This sense of contracted awareness in the head had loosened as a heart opening. This awareness beyond mind was alive with an intuitive intelligence that spoke in tones of silence and shades of transparent beauty—a simple, peaceful joy.

Yet there still remained a slight feeling of entering this awareness. However, as I sat with a photo of Mother Meera one night shortly after this, I had the feeling that it was time to go beyond. My body coursed with energy, as the top of my head felt like it was being rewired. With this came the subtle feeling of sinking back behind the witness. This could be described as more of a non-space than a space, but in reality it is beyond any idea of space or non-space. 'Infinitely magical' and 'divine' are but pale adjectives that may allude to it.

With this arose a clear seeing that nothing I could do, nor any plant I could work with, could bring me any closer to the divine presence that was already here. This awareness is the ground of being and it cannot be sought or found, as it is always ever-present. To look for it is to deny it, seeking is the turning from truth and the pretence that we are somehow separate. It was seen that there is no superior or inferior way, that whatever life presented at each moment was an expression of this awareness.

I had no need to find myself, seek visions, or wholeness. It was all already here and had always been here. Old spiritual patterns of becoming through plant work and shamanism began to crumble, as it was seen that awareness is not dependent upon anything. A deep gratitude was felt towards the plants as it was realised that the essence of the plants was this awareness and I was no other than this awareness. I cannot enter or leave this awareness, as I am this awareness. I was dying to all spirituality as an identity, or as a means of finding.

These patterns of 'me' and 'my' spirituality were like a wisp of thin smoke that hung in the air, giving the impression of a separate individual seeking—a phantom that the wind of truth dispels, revealing the transparent air of awareness—a vastness that, at all times, was the air. Awareness is never absent, just simply veiled by limitation, a temporary identification with form causing limited seeing. I could see that the work with the plants had been the winds of truth dispelling the illusion of separation, yet all had been the display of consciousness; smoke and wind were the one manifesting. Nothing had been amiss, 'I' truly had never been lost and, in reality, there had never been a separate individual undergoing healing, as the one and all were always already whole.

It was seen that the source of all is unbounded. This awareness, which could also be called Spirit, expresses itself as the manifestation of life in apparent multiplicity and diversity, as a display of plants, animals and elements—a continuum of becoming within consciousness. I was beginning to understand the source as a limitless potential, pregnant with infinite possibilities. It appears that formless awareness awakens to itself in the tasting of the spontaneously creative manifestation of form as the actualisation and objectification of pure potential. This creative force has no demands on manifestation and allows all to be as it appears. Even though there appears to be an evolution in form there is no end point to this evolution, as to have a goal would be a form of control. This creative impulse is the ultimate act of unconditional love and is the gift of true freedom without censure. This creativity is a perpetual joy unto itself, without beginning or end—a deep satisfaction as the source of being that is truly un-possessed.

As the foundations of my spiritual-seeking-through-plants gave way, I felt the tug of resistance to letting go of that which had been worked with for so long. This identity as a 'spiritual person' or 'plant healer' had a cohesion that needed to dissipate. This identity had, for so long, given a sense of security in being the doer. A feeling that I was on the path, that I was doing my best and that I was getting there. Yet all of this was the movement of a seemingly separate individual attempting to become whole or happy. This type of becoming can set the stage from cradle to grave, a trance of getting and purifying that perpetuates itself if we never stop to question who or what is the very 'I' undertaking such a path. The spiritual path has many dead ends or circular tracks that give the illusion of 'nearly there.' All the while we can be going around and around in circles, hungrily chasing our own tails. Spirituality itself can become a means to polish and refine the ego, giving one the feeling of moral superiority or righteousness, if we believe ourselves to have surpassed those we deem to be without spirituality or spiritual knowledge.

Then there are those who chase spiritual highs, visions and mystical states as a form of escapism, trying to avoid or escape life so as to reach a perfect fantasy of 'not here, not now.' Even the goal of awakening can be just the drive for a bigger and better 'me.' Yet the truth of awakening is humbling to the extreme. It is beyond all personal control or desire. There is nothing in it for the separate individual but its own demise.

Authentic spirituality questions from whence do we source our truth and from what position do we perceive. If we look to our own conditioned mind for the truth, we are then bound to unexamined ideologies and beliefs. The mind can be such a maze of confusing and contradictory thoughts. Yet it can be seen clearly by anyone, at any moment, that there appears to be someone or something that witnesses thoughts and feelings. If one can witness thoughts and feelings then one is not one's thoughts or feelings. To question the source of this witnessing is the love of truth and a questioning that cannot be answered by the intellectual mind. In fact, this questioning is the turning in of the mind, back upon itself; the cessation of outward flow of attention that then rests as the stillness and silence of not-knowing. It is this that dissolves the questioner. It is then that the intuitive, knowing awareness comes to the foreground as the taste of our true nature. Here the love of truth meets truth, collapsing all imagined boundaries in remembrance of the singularity of being. It is the beginning of the end of the divided personal world; it is to die before you die.

A spiritual path can be a wondrous journey but can also be a means to a refined identity wherein the very one undertaking such a path is not questioned. A time comes when we must look to ourselves and let no other become our authority. Any outer authority, whether that is a person, religion, or tradition can become an attachment to form and conceptual thinking that is a denial of the truth within. We must probe ourselves to find the inner teacher, the inner guru that is the truth and is no other. Other people may embody this truth but we must always look past their form to realise that what illuminates them, is illuminating everyone. The words of the Buddha echo this truth beautifully,

"Be a light unto yourself."

There is no other that can hand the truth to you; you must come to it directly in order to realise your true nature. In seeing 'no self' we see 'no other' and all is revealed to be an appearance of the divine.

One of the days, as I sat in our car at the local supermarket car park, I was once again overcome with the same un-possessed radiance that I had experienced at Mother Amma. As I looked out the window at the flow of people entering and leaving the store, I beheld the inner radiance of every person without exception as tears rolled down my cheek. There was an explosion of love and joy in my heart for the beauty of life in that moment. Whether it was an old, dishevelled farmer with cow dung on his boots, a young child with no front teeth, or a worried-looking mother, all I could see was their absolute beauty shining through.

These intense and ecstatic moments arose and were re-absorbed, but I was beginning to understand the importance of not attaching to any experience—pleasurable or not. For life is in a flow that delivers exactly what is required at any given moment.

I found that with an awakening and during the process of harmonisation afterwards, there can be accompanying feelings that are very beautiful and pleasurable. It can be easy to associate these feelings exclusively as being our true nature. Yet they too are but temporary expressions of the divine that are in no way superior to any other experiences, even though they may be closer in nature to wide open, infinite awareness. To cling to the pleasurable is to attempt to control the flow of manifestation. All experiences and phenomena, whether deemed pleasurable or not, are the manifestation of awareness as uncontrolled openness, an openness that has no opposite and that transcends all qualities in its emptiness.

More and more, these experiences gently shifted my perspective. I found that when I was chatting or engaged with people, I would find myself softly smiling inwardly as I could see a depth in all eyes that reminded me that whoever I was looking at was 'no other' than the divine itself in form, whether they were aware of it or not.

'I am' the love song of divinity

Coinciding with this deepening awareness was an absence; an absence that I would only come to know by the return of the awareness of objects. It was as if everything had disappeared and I only recognised this disappearance by the re-appearance of the world. It did not happen often and was not solicited. I could be doing some work when I would notice that there had been an absence. Like the feeling after emerging from deep sleep when, upon awakening, the world seems to re-weave itself. In such a case, one would know that one had been asleep, even though one could not say what had transpired. There would be no memory of anything having happened, as there would be nothing to reference—as opposed to the waking and dreaming states of consciousness wherein there is a constant display of feelings, sensations and thoughts that give one a sense of existence.

Yet these absences had a different quality, as there was no sense of having been asleep and they would happen in the middle of doing something. I also noticed that my dream state of consciousness had taken on a pronounced lucidity in this period. In one such dream, I knew I was dreaming and what came to me in that dream, as an intuitive knowing, was that the empty space within the dream and the objects of the dream were the one substance. It was seen within the dream that the entirety of the dream was one 'dream substance.' There was nothing separate within the dream; it was all dream consciousness. There was no empty space within the dream as it was all the one appearance, there was no movement within the dream as there was no space to move through and there was no time within the dream as time was the measurement of movement through space.

As this was seen in the dream state, I awoke to waking consciousness with the same knowing. I looked around the bedroom as everything took on a transparency and even the space between objects had a fullness. Everything took on an intimacy as all that was perceived was seen to be a seamless display of inner beauty without exclusion, where the conceptual constraints of time and space gave way to the totality of being. I lay back and watched the sleeping form of my wife and marvelled that there was absolutely no distance between us, as all was the one pervading consciousness. The sense of being awake within a dream had transposed to the waking state and the perfume of this still permeates. I was beginning to see that ultimately there is not a waking consciousness, a sleeping consciousness and a dreaming consciousness. There is waking, sleeping and dreaming which all unfolds in the one, natural, ever-present state of consciousness.

When we are within a dream we take it to be so real. In it we run, swim, laugh, fight and love with the full gamut of emotions, thoughts and sensations available. Yet upon waking from the dream, we claim it was all just a dream and not real, even though we may have had the pants scared off us! We awake from the dream and find that we are not the kings, villains, or lovers we had dreamed ourselves to be. We say it was just the imagination, or the processing of the psyche, but within the dream we were totally identified with our role and form.

It is somewhat like this when we begin to awaken to our true nature, when it is seen that there is no separate, personal self, that the little 'me' is but a limited identification with thoughts, feelings and sensations—a consortium of objects that we hold ourselves to be.

However, just as there is identification with the limited form of body-mind and associated thoughts and perceptions, there is also the possibility of dis-identification—withdrawal from the belief and feeling of being a separate individual. This process is underway when we begin to witness our thoughts, feelings and sensations. For anything that can be witnessed is an object and so not what we truly are as the subject. We begin to see ourselves as the witness of these objects. We may not be able to describe or agree upon what this witness is, but we all have the knowledge or awareness of the reality of being—of the 'I am.' For our own existence is so self-evident, that to even try to deny that 'I am' is the very assertion and validation of it. One must first 'be' to make any such a claim or denial.

This knowledge of 'I am' can feel very personal from the standpoint of the separate individual. However, I came to see that this personal 'I am' is the heart-knot of ignorance, the identification of limitless consciousness with a limited form, the body-mind as a pseudo-subject. This 'I am' is the root of all becoming: 'I am a man,' 'I am a mechanic,' 'I am a priest,' 'I am angry,' 'I am rich.' This contraction of consciousness to a limited form is felt as a lack, a move from wholeness to division; a lack that drives the constant need to become in an effort to make whole that lack—the desire for desirelessness. This is the dynamism of craving and aversion as a means to become whole and happy in a world of division, where the very momentum to become sustains the belief in being a separate, isolated individual.

Nevertheless, at some stage this momentum loses pace and the world of glittering objects loses its shine. One may get a glimpse of unity or begin to question, 'What is it all about?' which starts the process of reorientation. As we question this idea of personal self, 'Who or what am I?' there may come a seeing of the truth of 'no-self.' Self-Realisation may be sudden or gradual, total or partial, nonetheless the stage is set for the dis-identification of consciousness from a limited form. It is a return journey to the natural state, a state that we have never really left, as all unfolds in and as consciousness.

This seeing of 'no-self' expands the personal 'I am' to an impersonal and universal 'I am,' an 'I am' that is the entirety of manifestation that arises from the wordless, un-manifest 'I.' This may be a total and permanent shift, or an ebb and flow that harmonises to a rhythm beyond control.

I found, more and more, that I came to rest in and as this 'I am'-ness, as if it was pulling the remaining strands of personal 'me' back into the tapestry of being.

All attention that had been focused on personal becoming had turned to face the source, the root of manifestation, the 'I am.'

Pondering Possibilities

If there is only one, can there be any God to blame?
If there is only one, can there be any other to blame?

If there is only one, can there be any hurting of another?
If there is only one, can there be any loving of another?

If there is only one, can there be any control of expression?
If there is only one, can there be any denial of experience?

If there is only one, can there be any absence of the one?
If there is only one, can there be any bondage of the one?

If there is only one, can there be any wrong one?
If there is only one, can there be any right one?

If there is only one, can there be any you plus one?
If there is only one, can there be any me plus one?

If there is only one, can there be only one?

Nothing is as it appears

This abiding as 'I am' deepened over months. It brought about many beautiful and joyful insights, along with the challenge of deeper surrender, mentally, emotionally and physically. It was not simply a matter of intellectually understanding 'I am,' it was in the resting as it, that there came a transcendent transparency.

Letting go of the personal 'I am' often felt like a death, as personal hopes and dreams were let go of. This loss of personal will and control was sometimes felt quite physically as energetic jolts within the body, especially at the heart and solar plexus. It was as if a sledgehammer was pounding on my stomach, the beat of non-existence that countered 'my' held, personal existence.

This became quite pronounced as there was a further letting go that could be described as a pull beyond the 'I am.' This movement felt like 'I' was being taken back, prior to the 'I am.' 'I' as pure subjectivity without the 'am.' Absolutely nothing can be said of this Ultimate 'I,' for to describe something one must be able to know it through observation. The Ultimate 'I' is pure subjectivity, so can never be seen or found. It is the mysterious unknown and 'I am that.' More and more, the reality of this was established as the 'such-ness' of life, life as the spontaneous awareness of itself exactly as it is. At this time, which was shortly after my last visit to Mother Meera, I awoke from sleep one night with my body a mass of scintillating energy as if I was on fire. I heard the words,

"The Self can never be touched."

Many resistances to this unknown played themselves out over this period. One of the last was a slippery fish indeed. It came as the thought that I was not quite there yet and came over me as the feeling that there was still something missing—something crucial. It was the feeling-belief that 'I' was still somehow bound and with this came the urge to find a solution, so as to find a way out of this bondage.

I came to within a hair's breadth of moving with this urge to seek. Instead, I simply sat down and opened to this sense of lack and wrongness, whereas before I would have assumed doer-ship and worked to tackle the problem. Now I just sat in openness, hour after hour, as waves of frustration attempted to pull me along with this sense of non-rightness. On and on it rolled with a sense of utter defeat. Then it clicked, it was seen that under these thoughts and feelings of wrongness was the belief that it should not be this way, that these feelings and thoughts should not be here and that I needed to get rid of them. This had been seen to some degree before, but this time the very visceral sense of it was showing itself as the hidden judge that desired to control and avoid what it deemed as not worthy.

It was easy to embrace the beauty of life but awareness does not resist anything. It was the embracing of the ugly and unwanted as equally valid that was vital. I could see that 'I' was beyond any positive or negative thoughts, emotions, sensations—beyond all interrelated opposites. What had arisen to be seen was the old, remaining, seeking pattern of spirituality.

There was a spontaneous flash, where the 'I' stood apart, looking in the mirror of 'I am,' the seed of manifestation. 'I' became aware of itself: self-conscious. It was appreciated that the 'I,' absolute subjectivity, has a propensity to manifests itself and in so doing comes to know itself—for no reason other than its nature is a creative impulse which eternally expresses and experiences all of itself.

With this transparency of truth there was no elation, no success and nothing gained. All I could do was smile and laugh at the simplicity of it all: a playful cosmic game as the one hides from itself in time and space. I had always been what I was looking for. I had never been lost or incomplete. I had never not been what I am.

I knew that, in this life, there may be illness, grief, anger, wealth, pleasure, or pain, but I could see that there was nothing personal in it and there was nothing amiss. I am beyond, yet I see myself in all. There was absolutely no question of a separate person in bondage and in corollary, there was seen to be no liberation for this illusory separate person either.

I am not lost nor am I gained,
I am not bound nor am I found
I am not two as I am you
And as you I am all
In this mirror I shine
A reality within a dream
Both beyond and within
I am

In this seeing, there was a simple surety of a peaceful joy without cause. A bliss in the 'such-ness' of each moment that was not dependent upon circumstances.

A couple of days later, I took my shamanic drums and rattle to a field and buried them without thought or ritual, a spontaneous action without any sense of loss. Although I had not used these tools for eight to nine months since the seeing of 'no-self,' they had been tools I had used and cherished for many years. Yet there had remained a slight holding on to them as an identification, for what would I be without them?

With this seeing though, I had died to spirituality as anything 'other.' Shamanism as an identity or a means to find or heal the psychological self was no more. This is not to disavow shamanism—there is a great skill and beauty to it as a technique of discovery and as a celebration of the wonder of life in the conscious expression of our true nature. But shamanism as I had known it had fallen away, much like a ripe fruit.

Awakening could be said to be the cessation of the illusion of psychological suffering of a separate individual who has been seeking happiness, wholeness, or God.

Here is where I find 'I am,' nothing more and nothing less. There is a deepening underway, a maturing, as old body-mind patterns are no longer identified with as a limitation to overcome, but are recognised as no other than an expression of divine consciousness in a specific form—a form that in essence is not separate. Here wisdom arises in the embracing of all aspects of humanity, a willingness to embody awakening, as the infinite potential awakens all of itself in the world of form—an act of unconditional love.

For the truth must not only be realised but also expressed as a harmonisation beyond personal control in the ending of all division or divisiveness—a transmutation that liberates all human patterns in the embrace of no other. This is not to suggest that everything is not already ultimately harmonious, but simply that one becomes more aware of it as one rests back as open, clear awareness.

Perhaps there is no end to the deepening of realisation, as there may always be more to be seen. Yet there is now a 'satisfactoriness' in not knowing what is in store, as herein lies the beauty of discovery coupled with an appreciation that all is already in hand in the yoga of being and becoming.

Our heart

The 'I am' is where all minds reach their limit, as the mind is of the relative world of the knowable. In a mind-made world of craving and aversion there is a veritable feast of diversity and multiplicity to be tasted and explored. Yet all desires within the world of objects can be boiled down to the one basic desire, the desire for happiness and peace—deep satisfaction. It is a desire that can be sought in many forms: politics, materialism, love, spirituality, adventure, or power. Yet all are based on the acquiring or losing of something that will bring about this happiness and peace, which is, in essence, the cessation of desire itself. It is remarkable to see that the primary desire of all people is to be desire-less.

Anything that can be gained in the mind-made world of division and impermanence can be lost. Hence any personal desire fulfilled within the relative world is fleeting and cannot bring about permanent happiness and peace. This is seen, time and time again, in that when we acquire the objects of our desire there is a temporary satisfaction for a period of time: minutes, weeks, years, or decades. But then we either become dissatisfied with the object, or we lose the object. When we become dissatisfied with the object there is felt a restlessness which gives rise to yet another desire to acquire in the movement of becoming. In the case of losing the object, whether it is through loss, theft, death, or decay, there is also a dissatisfaction of no longer having the happiness and peace that it had brought. There then follows a longing desire to have it back, or a desire for something to replace it.

Again and again, we seek to fulfil desire in the relative world of form, which by its very nature is impermanent. Lasting satisfaction, happiness and peace cannot be found there, only the perpetuation of cycles of gain and loss in the play of duality. Here though, impermanence can be seen to be a blessing in that it can orientate one back to that which is permanent.

When we thoroughly investigate desire we find that it is the desire for desire-less-ness that is the goal and the reward, it itself is the truth of permanent happiness and peace. It is being without wanting and presence without seeking, in which the 'I' is no longer in the act of seeking itself as happiness and peace in an external, relative world of objects.

A time may come when we become disillusioned and recognise that the striving for satisfaction in the mind-made world is an endless cycle of 'I got it' and 'I lost it.' Here is where we may start to question the nature of our perceived existence as a separate individual. This is a turning around—a willingness to know Reality. The love of truth becomes our inner compass. An irresistible urge to the source is felt as a natural homecoming. We face ourselves with the question,

"Who or what am I?"

We now seek the source of 'I am' and our own separate self-existence is called into question. The mind turns back in on itself. The questioner is questioned with the unbending love of truth. A relentless opening to truth where the long-held identification with the psychological self begins to give way in the silence of not knowing. Here the unknown strips clean the layers of 'me' and 'mine' to reveal the naked truth that happiness and peace is without beginning or end.

It would appear that an effort or choice is needed to turn within and face the seeming veil of separation. Yet at those moments when clarity and awareness pre-veil there is an effortlessness that sings without choice. A being without the need to know, resting in a deep satisfaction without reason or purpose. At these moments life is a seamless, ever-present expression of an unchanging, unseen spirit—a dance beyond existence and non-existence as the pulse and breath of manifestation.

I can see the magnetism of truth was always at play in so many aspects of my life, silently welcoming and allowing all to be. In nature it was felt as a gentle peace that at times would mirror a deeper, formless stillness beyond conditioned body-mind patterns, while in art there was a taste of timelessness experienced in the looking and crafting as the creative presence without ownership. In singing it was experienced as the surrender to a flow of expression, as the beauty of living without control, where the 'me' would give way to the moment, dying in the constant birth of what 'is.'

All the while the vibrational essence of the plants loosened the limiting beliefs of 'me' and 'other' in a world of division. The psychological and somatic threads of past experience that gave credence to the 'me' faded in the clear light of awareness. The plants, as an expression of the divine, held a key to unlock the limiting, illusory structures of separateness, dissolving the veil until it was seen that the true essence of the plants was not different than my own essence—the one essence in a multitude of undivided forms.

As I came to see the essence of all in one and one in all, I found that no outer prop was necessary for happiness. To open to our inherent nature, there is no prescription, no defined set of steps, or no single way—all is consciousness and consciousness flowers in accordance with the uniqueness of each of its own manifestations. No two awakenings are the same, as no two sets of conditions are the same. It is not so important to mimic the outer movement of awakening as it is to simply turn within in openness. In this openness there is the relinquishment of control and outward seeking, a movement from 'my will' to 'thy will.' As, in truth, the belief in control of the fictitious 'me' is but an egoic spin of denial that is the mere holding of separation with the after-thought that I am the separate thinker and doer.

In life we all have these homing beacons, windows into eternity that are expansions beyond the limited, personal self. Moments of great joy, beauty and love, where we temporarily lose our limited 'me-ness,' precious and timeless glimpses of our inherent nature as limitless awareness. Often, after such moments, the egoic-mind may rush in to own, label, or deny what is unpossessable and indescribable—a vain attempt at control and defence. Yet at no time has what we truly are been tarnished or left, our home ground always 'is.' It is like the empty space around you that allows you and this book to be.

Awareness is openness without agenda, a clear and transparent emptiness that is welcoming beyond measure. With it there is no conflict with what 'is,' as what 'is' is of itself and no other. Awareness manifests as the appearance of arising and falling forms within itself, yet awareness has never been changed or touched—it is already and always whole.

Spirit is having the human experience and this humanness is not separate from the divinity that we are. The recognition and living of this realisation is the embodiment of awakening expressing itself uniquely through the body-mind as the actualisation of Spirit in time and space.

When we embrace our humanness with the realisation of no-self, then what we are as unique, undivided individuals is seen to be a creative expression of the oneness that is at the heart of our being.

I share with you some of the movements of my life, not because they were important in and of themselves, but as pointers they may serve as a remembrance to our inherent nature beyond all stories. For all words are of relative reality, doomed to fail in describing the indescribable. Yet the source of these words and the space between these words are a silent, gateless gate of welcoming.

From the absolute perspective, this book and all books are but a fiction, a story that may or may not point clearly to the source. There is great beauty and challenge in questioning who we are without our stories. To pare things down to the essential truth of silence is a falling away of all, rather than a path to be followed—a trackless field beyond right and wrong where being and becoming are non-separate.

On the last occasion that I got to sit with Mother Meera in darshan I heard the words,

"Our Heart"

The plural and the singular.
I found these words funnelled attention back to the 'I am.'
Our shared source of one heart.
They are offered from no other.

Author's Note

A word to the wise, I feel it is important to elucidate upon the use of sacred plant medicines to the neophyte. Although sacred plant medicines are revered in some cultures and countries, in others they can be misunderstood and demonised. So I would advise you to make yourself fully aware as to the legality regarding the use of any plant medicine within your country.

Also it is important and perhaps vital, that one undertake any usage under the tutelage and guidance of an experienced plant master, or a trained professional. Few are called to work with plant medicines and fewer still to work by themselves with the plants. The path of plant medicine work is not without its dangers and pitfalls, but with a true and clear guide, one may experience the depth, beauty and healing that the plant world has to offer.

A good teacher will also assess the suitability of each person as to their capacity to work with the plant medicines, as it may not be suitable for some people with certain physical predispositions or psychological disorders.

My own personal work with mapacho, psilocybin and ayahuasca plant medicines came to a close some time back as I no longer feel the need to find or fix myself. Neither do I feel called to guide people in the use of these plants, nor do I recommend any specific teachers. The resonance and pull towards any teacher is a matter of the head, heart and gut and is best felt from within, when adequate research on a specific plant and teacher has been undertaken.

The path of the plants is no sure-fire way to awakening, it is but one path among many—and no path is better than another. Yet when the plants themselves are seen to be sacred, then they may reflect back to us our own sacredness. We may then come to realise that all of life is the appearance of divinity and we are that, a flow of life that knows no right or wrong and whose heart is open to all as one. This is where all paths lead, until we come to see that no path is necessary, as we are already home.

For more information, please visit
www.embracingnoother.com

Printed in Great Britain
by Amazon.co.uk, Ltd.,
Marston Gate.